ISBN 978-1-331-06018-5
PIBN 10139587

1 MONTH OF
FREE
READING

at

www.ForgottenBooks.com

By purchasing this book you are eligible for one month membership to ForgottenBooks.com, giving you unlimited access to our entire collection of over 700,000 titles via our web site and mobile apps.

To claim your free month visit:

www.forgottenbooks.com/free139587

English
Français
Deutsche
Italiano
Español
Português

www.forgottenbooks.com

Mythology Photography **Fiction**
Fishing Christianity **Art** Cooking
Essays Buddhism Freemasonry
Medicine **Biology** Music **Ancient**
Egypt Evolution Carpentry Physics
Dance Geology **Mathematics** Fitness
Shakespeare **Folklore** Yoga Marketing
Confidence Immortality Biographies
Poetry **Psychology** Witchcraft
Electronics Chemistry History **Law**
Accounting **Philosophy** Anthropology
Alchemy Drama Quantum Mechanics
Atheism Sexual Health **Ancient History**
Entrepreneurship Languages Sport
Paleontology Needlework Islam
Metaphysics Investment Archaeology
Parenting Statistics Criminology
Motivational

from

JAMES BOSWELL'S

L I F E

of

SAMUEL JOHNSON

CHOSEN and EDITED

B Y

R. W. CHAPMAN, M.A., R.G.A.

O X F O R D

At the CLARENDON PRESS

M DCCCC XXI

Which of us but remembers . . . the day when he opened these airy volumes, fascinating him by a true natural magic! It was as if the curtains of the past were drawn aside, and we looked mysteriously into a kindred country, where dwelt our Fathers; inexpressibly dear to us, but which had seemed forever hidden from our eyes.

CARLYLE.

PRINTED IN ENGLAND.

PREFACE

THE rising generation is, it may be feared, better acquainted with Macaulay's travesty of Boswell and of Johnson than with the great originals which he so flagrantly traduced. Boswell's book is very long (it contains more than half a million words); large parts of it assume familiarity with Latin; and the beginning of the book is much less attractive than the rest. The present editor, who attacked it at a tender age, was deterred partly by the perplexing mass of Croker's notes, partly also by the long quotations and lists of conjectural attributions; and after wandering for a space in those crepuscular regions, forsook the journey before the sun was up.

If any apology is required for making a selection from a work in its nature discontinuous, the authority may be cited of Johnson himself; who was at first angry with Bishop Hurd for publishing a mutilated Cowley, but afterwards relenting allowed that 'there is no impropriety in a man's publishing as much as he chooses of any authour, if he does not put the rest out of the way'.

Many of the pieces here printed are what no selector could resist; but the compiler has tried to withstand

the temptation to quote all the most brilliant apo-
phthegms and pungent sallies, which would be to give
a false impression of the book. He has tried to make
such a selection as will give, within its limits, what
the book itself gives so incomparably, a true picture
of Johnson's character and of the Johnsonian circle.
To this end are included specimens of Johnson's letters
and anecdotes of his acquaintance, as well as a
number of pieces by Boswell and others, which last
are not in themselves gems of literature.

The fame of Johnson's talk, and the formal elabora-
tion of his written style, have given rise to a notion—
from which even his contemporaries were not free—
that his writing was but a laboured and turgid ex-
pansion of his oral wisdom. *Johnsonese* means poly-
syllabic pomp. The extracts from his letters and
occasional writings should correct this error.

Johnson needs neither apology nor eulogy. But
Boswell so frequently exposes himself to ridicule, and
has been so cruelly mishandled by critics, that his
admirers may be allowed to speak in his defence.
Macaulay's paradox, that Boswell was able to write
one of the greatest of all books because he was an
exceptionally bad and foolish man, perhaps hardly
deserves to be refuted. Yet Macaulay's picture of
Boswell was so vividly drawn that it made an impression which is not yet effaced. Carlyle, while he
rejected the 'strange hypothesis' that it was 'the very
fact of his being among the worst men in this world

that had enabled him to write one of the best books therein', pulled down one paradox only to set up another: that 'the babbling Bozzy,[1] inspired only by love, and the recognition and vision which love can lend ... unconsciously works together for us a whole Johnsoniad'. This is not only absurd; no amount of veneration could have given Boswell his extraordinary powers of memory, his lucid, pleasant English, or his rare dramatic sense of character and of a scene; it is also gratuitously absurd. There is no reason to suppose that Boswell was ·a 'welter of terrestrial dross'. The evidence is all against it. A man excessively vicious and excessively foolish would not have been described as 'a man whom every body likes' nor as 'the best travelling companion in the world'; would not have lived as the intimate of such men as Burke, Beauclerk, Reynolds, Lord Hailes and General Oglethorpe; nor died (as Malone tells us) 'to the great regret of all his friends'. Boswell's moral and intellectual failings were sufficiently obvious to his contemporaries, and are still more glaring to us from the open simplicity with which he exposes his vanities and follies. But his virtues of head and heart are equally patent to any one who reads his book without preconception.

Boswell wrote his own character in his *Tour to the*

---

[1] *Babbling Bozzy* contains a *suggestio falsi*; Johnson shortened all his friends' names, as *Lanky, Goldy*. *Bozzy* was a term, not of contempt, but of affection.

Hebrides: 'I have given a sketch of Dr. Johnson: my readers may wish to know a little of his fellow traveller. Think then, of a gentleman of ancient blood, the pride of which was his predominant passion. He was then in his thirty-third year, and had been about four years happily married. His inclination was to be a soldier; but his father, a respectable Judge, had pressed him into the service of the law. He had thought more than any body supposed, and had a pretty good stock of general learning and knowledge. He had all Dr. Johnson's principles, with some degree of relaxation. He had rather too little, than too much prudence; and, his imagination being lively, he often said things of which the effect was different from the intention.'

R. W. C.

MACEDONIA,
June 1918.

NOTE

(*The references are to the numbers of the extracts.*)

SAMUEL JOHNSON was born at Lichfield on 18 September 1709 (5) Educated at Lichfield School and at Stourbridge. Commoner of Pembroke College Oxford 31 Oct. 1728 (6). Left Oxford Autumn 1731. His father died Dec. 1731. Usher at Market-Bosworth School July 1732. Went to Birmingham, where he translated Lobo's *Voyage to Abyssinia* (published 1735). Returned to Lichfield 1734. Married Mrs. Elizabeth Porter, a widow of forty-eight, 1735. Set up a private academy at Edial near Lichfield, 1736 (9). Began his tragedy *Irene*. Went to London with his pupil David Garrick, March 1737 (10), and in the following autumn settled with Mrs. Johnson in London, where he continued to live, mostly in the neighbourhood of Fleet Street, until his death. Became a regular contributor to the *Gentleman's Magazine*, for which he wrote the Parliamentary Debates (12). Published *London, a Poem*, May 1738 (13). *Life of Richard Savage*, Feb. 1744. *Prospectus* of a Dictionary of the English Language, addressed to the Earl of Chesterfield, 1747 (14). *The Vanity of Human Wishes*, Jan. 1749. *Irene* produced by Garrick, and published, Feb. 1749. *The Rambler*, twice weekly, March 1750–March 1752. His wife died 17 March 1752 (15). Became acquainted with Bennet Langton Esq. and Topham Beauclerk Esq. (16). Letter to Lord Chesterfield, Feb. 1755 (17) Made Master of Arts of the University of Oxford by diploma, 1755. The Dictionary published (18). Proposals for an edition of Shakespeare, 1756 (22). *The Idler*, every Saturday, 15 April 1758 – 5 April 1760. His mother died, Jan. 1759 (23). To 'defray the expence of his mother's funeral, and pay some little debts which she had left' he wrote *Rasselas, Prince of Abyssinia* in the evenings of one week (*Life*, 1759). Received from the Crown a pension of £300 a year, 1762 (24). Met Boswell, 16 May 1763 (25). Goldsmith's *Vicar of Wakefield* (31). The CLUB, afterwards called the Literary Club, proposed by Mr. Joshua Reynolds and founded 1764 (44). Introduced to the Thrales, 1765 (47). Made Doctor of Laws by Trinity College Dublin, 1765. His edition of Shakespeare published, Oct. 1765. Conversation with George III, 1767 (50). *The False Alarm*, pamphlet on the Middlesex Election, 1770. *Thoughts on the late Transactions respecting Falkland's Islands*, pamphlet advocating peace, 1771. Visited Scotland with Boswell, Aug.–Nov. 1773 (78). *Journey to the Western Islands of Scotland*, 1775. Doctor of Civil Law of the University of Oxford, 1775 (87). *Taxation No Tyranny*, pamphlet against the American claims, 1775. Visited France with the Thrales, 1775. In the last twenty years of his life Johnson published relatively little except the *Lives of the Poets*; and the second half of Boswell's *Life* consists almost entirely of his letters and talk. Four volumes of *Prefaces, Biographical and Critical, to the Works of the English Poets* (better known by their later title of *Lives of the most Eminent English Poets*) published 1779; the remaining six, 1781 (125). Died 13 Dec. 1784 (205–207).

Of Johnson's writings other than the *Dictionary*, *Ramblers* and *Idlers* may still be found in second-hand shops; but most readers prefer to taste those effusions in small doses as provided by the contemporary *Beauties of Johnson* or modern anthologies of British Essays. The *Preface to Shakespeare* is printed in Mr. D. Nichol Smith's collection *Eighteenth Century Essays on Shakespeare*, and (with the *Proposals* and a selection from the *Notes* chosen by Sir Walter Raleigh) in the *Oxford Library of Prose and Poetry*. Early editions of the *Lives of the Poets* are very common and cheap.

The standard Library edition of the *Lives* and of Johnsoniana is that of Dr. Birkbeck Hill (Clarendon Press). The thirteen volumes include, besides the *Lives* and Boswell's *Life* and *Tour*, two volumes of *Letters* and two of *Miscellanies* selected from Mrs. Piozzi's *Anecdotes*, Sir John Hawkins's *Life*, and many other sources.

Of recent writers on Johnson the most eminent is Sir Walter Raleigh, whose *Six Essays on Johnson* (Clarendon Press) are full of wisdom and humanity.

JAMES BOSWELL was born at Auchinleck (Affleck) in Ayrshire, 1740. His father was a landowner and a Scottish judge, and as such bore the title of Lord Auchinleck. Educated at the Universities of Edinburgh and Glasgow.

Introduced to Johnson 16 May 1763 (25). Left Harwich for Utrecht to study the law, Aug. 1763 (42). Travelled on the continent and visited Corsica. Returned to London Feb. 1766. Admitted an advocate (Edinburgh). 1766. *Account of Corsica*, 1768 (54). *British Essays in favour of the Brave Corsicans, collected and published by J. B.*, 1769. Married Margaret Montgomerie 'my very valuable wife', 1769. Elected to the Club 1773 (73).

Boswell came to London from Scotland 1768, 69, 72, 73, 75, 76, 78, 79 (twice), 81, 83, 84, and was with Johnson at Dr. Taylor's (Ashbourne) in 1776 and 77.

Journal of a Tour to the Hebrides, 1785 (78 and note).

The Life of Samuel Johnson, LL.D., 1791. In the *Advertisement* Boswell acknowledges his debt to his 'friend Mr. Malone, who was so good as to allow me to read to him almost the whole of my manuscript'. Many additions were made in the second edition (1793), and the author was revising the book for a third edition at his death (19 May 1795). The third edition (1799) was accordingly superintended by Malone, who made further additions and corrections in the fourth, fifth, and sixth editions.

The present selection follows the text of the third edition. The third is substantially the 'last lifetime' edition; though Boswell did not live to see it published, it contained all his latest additions and corrections; and we can trust Malone as we trust Boswell. The accuracy of the text was ascertained by Birkbeck Hill, who compared it with the earlier editions.

The text here printed, unless otherwise indicated, is either Boswell, or if in inverted commas Johnson quoted by Boswell. The foot-notes printed with the text are Boswell's, unless the name of the writer (usually Malone) is appended. Any connecting links (other than the headings) which it seemed necessary to insert in the text are 'enclosed within crochets' after Malone's example. To each extract is prefixed the date under which it appears in Boswell; this will enable the reader to trace the passage to its place in any complete edition.

CONTENTS

C O N T E N T S xvii

ILLUSTRATIONS

OF

SAMUEL JOHNSON, LL.D.

COMPREHENDING

AN ACCOUNT OF HIS STUDIES

AND NUMEROUS WORKS,

IN CHRONOLOGICAL ORDER;

A SERIES OF HIS EPISTOLARY CORRESPONDENCE

AND CONVERSATIONS WITH MANY EMINENT PERSONS;

AND

VARIOUS ORIGINAL PIECES OF HIS COMPOSITION,

NEVER BEFORE PUBLISHED:

THE WHOLE EXHIBITING A VIEW OF LITERATURE AND
LITERARY MEN IN GREAT-BRITAIN, FOR NEAR
HALF A CENTURY, DURING WHICH HE
FLOURISHED.

By *JAMES BOSWELL*, Esq

——————— *Quò fit ut* OMNIS
Votiva pateat veluti descripta tabella
VITA SENIS.————   HORAT.

THE THIRD EDITION, REVISED AND AUGMENTED,

IN FOUR VOLUMES.

———

VOLUME THE FIRST.

———

LONDON:

PRINTED BY H. BALDWIN AND SON,

FOR CHARLES DILLY, IN THE POULTRY.

———

MDCCXCIX.

2. *From the Dedication to Sir Joshua Reynolds.*

My Dear Sir,—Every liberal motive that can actuate an Authour in the dedication of his labours, concurs in directing me to you, as the person to whom the following Work should be inscribed.

If there be a pleasure in celebrating the distinguished merit of a contemporary, mixed with a certain degree of vanity not altogether inexcusable, in appearing fully sensible of it, where can I find one, in complimenting whom I can with more general approbation gratify those feelings? Your excellence not only in the Art over which you have long presided with unrivalled fame, but also in Philosophy and elegant Literature, is well known to the present, and will continue to be the admiration of future ages. Your equal and placid temper, your variety of conversation, your true politeness, by which you are so amiable in private society, and that enlarged hospitality which has long made your house a common centre of union for the great, the accomplished, the learned, and the ingenious; all these qualities I can, in perfect confidence of not being accused of flattery, ascribe to you.

If a man may indulge an honest pride, in having it known to the world, that he has been thought worthy of particular attention by a person of the first eminence in the age in which he lived, whose company has been universally courted, I am justified in availing myself of the usual privilege of a Dedication, when I mention that there has been a long and uninterrupted friendship between us.

If gratitude should be acknowledged for favours received, I have this opportunity, my dear Sir, most sincerely to thank you for the many happy hours which I owe to your kindness,—for the cordiality with which you have at all times been pleased to welcome me,—for the number of valuable acquaintances to whom you have introduced me,—for the *noctes cœnœque Deûm*, which I have enjoyed under your roof.

If a work should be inscribed to one who is master of the subject of it, and whose approbation, therefore, must ensure it credit and success, the Life of Dr. Johnson is, with the greatest propriety, dedicated to Sir Joshua Reynolds, who was the intimate and beloved friend of that great man; the friend, whom he declared to be 'the most invulnerable man he knew; whom, if he should quarrel with him, he should find the most difficulty how to abuse.' You, my dear Sir, studied him, and knew him well: you venerated and admired him. Yet, luminous as he was upon the whole, you perceived all the shades which mingled in the grand composition; all the little peculiarities and slight blemishes which marked the literary Colossus. Your very warm commendation of the specimen which I gave in my 'Journal of a Tour to the Hebrides', of my being able to preserve his conversation in an authentick and lively manner, which opinion the Publick has confirmed, was the best encouragement for me to persevere in my purpose of producing the whole of my stores. . . . .

I am, my dear Sir,
Your much obliged friend,
And faithful humble servant,
JAMES BOSWELL.

London,
April 20, 1791. *not hampered by.......... astute!?*

3. *From the Advertisement to the Second Edition.*

It seems to me, in my moments of self-complacency, that this extensive biographical work, however inferior in its nature, may in one respect be assimilated to the *Odyssey*. Amidst a thousand entertaining and instructive episodes the *Hero* is never long out of sight; for they are all in some degree connected with him; and *He*, in the whole course of the History, is exhibited by the Authour for the best advantage of his readers.

'—Quid virtus et quid sapientia possit,
Utile proposuit nobis exemplar Ulyssen.'...

There are some men, I believe, who have, or think they have, a very small share of vanity. Such may speak of their literary fame in a decorous style of diffidence. But I confess, that I am so formed by nature and by habit, that to restrain the effusion of delight, on having obtained such fame, to me would be truly painful. Why then should I suppress it? Why 'out of the abundance of the heart' should I not speak? Let me then mention with a warm, but no insolent exultation, that I have been regaled with spontaneous praise of my work by many and various persons eminent for their rank, learning, talents and accomplishments; much of which praise I have under their hands to be reposited in my archives at *Auchinleck.* An honourable and reverend friend speaking of the favourable reception of my volumes, even in the circles of fashion and elegance, said to me, 'you have made them all talk Johnson,'—Yes, I may add, I have *Johnsonised* the land; and I trust they will not only *talk,* but *think,* Johnson.

4. *Introductory.*

To write the Life of him who excelled all mankind in writing the lives of others, and who, whether we consider his extraordinary endowments, or his various works, has been equalled by few in any age, is an arduous, and may be reckoned in me a presumptuous task.

Had Dr. Johnson written his own life, in conformity with the opinion which he has given [1], that every man's life may be best written by himself; had he employed in the preservation of his own history, that clearness of narration and elegance of language in which he has embalmed so many eminent persons, the world would probably have had the most perfect example of biography that was ever exhibited. But although he at different times, in a desultory manner, committed to writing many particulars of the progress of his mind and fortunes, he never had persevering diligence enough to form them into a regular composition. Of these memorials a few have been preserved; but the greater

---

[1] *Idler,* No. 84.

part was consigned by him to the flames, a few days before his death.

As I had the honour and happiness of enjoying his friendship for upwards of twenty years; as I had the scheme of writing his life constantly in view; as he was well apprised of this circumstance, and from time to time obligingly satisfied my inquiries, by communicating to me the incidents of his early years; as I acquired a facility in recollecting, and was very assiduous in recording, his conversation, of which the extraordinary vigour and vivacity constituted one of the first features of his character; and as I have spared no pains in obtaining materials concerning him, from every quarter where I could discover that they were to be found, and have been favoured with the most liberal communications by his friends; I flatter myself that few biographers have entered upon such a work as this, with more advantages; independent of literary abilities, in which I am not vain enough to compare myself with some great names who have gone before me in this kind of writing. . . . .

Instead of melting down my materials into one mass, and constantly speaking in my own person, by which I might have appeared to have more merit in the execution of the work, I have resolved to adopt and enlarge upon the excellent plan of Mr. Mason, in his Memoirs of Gray. Wherever narrative is necessary to explain, connect, and supply, I furnish it to the best of my abilities; but in the chronological series of Johnson's life, which I trace as distinctly as I can, year by year, I produce, wherever it is in my power, his own minutes, letters or conversation, being con-vinced that this mode is more lively, and will make my readers better acquainted with him, than even most of those were who actually knew him, but could know him only partially; whereas there is here an accumulation of intelligence from various points, by which his character is more fully understood and illustrated.

Indeed I cannot conceive a more perfect mode of writing any man's life, than not only relating all the most important events of it in their order, but inter-weaving what he privately wrote, and said, and thought; by which mankind are enabled as it were to see him live, and to ' live o'er each scene' with him, as he actually advanced through the several stages of his life. Had his other friends been as diligent and ardent as I was, he might have been almost entirely preserved. As it is, I will venture to say that he will be seen in this work more completely than any man who has ever yet lived.

And he will be seen as he really was; for I profess to write, not his panegyrick, which must be all praise, but his Life; which, great and good as he was, must not be supposed to be entirely perfect. To be as he was, is indeed subject of panegyrick enough to any man in this state of being; but in every picture there should be shade as well as light, and when I delineate him without reserve, I do what he himself recommended, both by his precept and his example.

5. *Birth and Parentage.*

SAMUEL JOHNSON was born at Lichfield, in Stafford-
shire, on the 18th of September, N.S., 1709; and his
initiation into the Christian church was not delayed;
for his baptism is recorded, in the register of St. Mary's
parish in that city, to have been performed on the day
of his birth. His father is there stiled *Gentleman*,
a circumstance of which an ignorant panegyrist has
praised him for not being proud; when the truth is,
that the appellation of Gentleman, though now lost in
the indiscriminate assumption of *Esquire*, was commonly taken by those who could not boast of gentility.
His father was Michael Johnson, a native of Derbyshire, of obscure extraction, who settled in Lichfield
as a bookseller and stationer.   His mother was Sarah
Ford, descended of an ancient race of substantial
yeomanry in Warwickshire. They were well advanced
in years when they married, and never had more than
two children, both sons; Samuel, their first born, who
lived to be the illustrious character whose various
excellence I am to endeavour to record, and Nathanael,
who died in his twenty-fifth year.

Mr. Michael Johnson was a man of a large and robust
body, and of a strong and active mind; yet, as in the
most solid rocks veins of unsound substance are often
discovered, there was in him a mixture of that disease,
the nature of which eludes the most minute enquiry,
though the effects are well known to be a weariness of
life, an unconcern about those things which agitate
the greater part of mankind, and a general sensation

of gloomy wretchedness. From him then his son inherited, with some other qualities, 'a vile melancholy,' which in his too strong expression of any disturbance of the mind, 'made him mad all his life, at least not sober.' Michael was, however, forced by the narrowness of his circumstances to be very diligent in business, not only in his shop, but by occasionally resorting to several towns in the neighbourhood, some of which were at a considerable distance from Lichfield. At that time booksellers' shops in the provincial towns of England were very rare, so that there was not one even in Birmingham, in which town old Mr. Johnson used to open a shop every market-day. He was a pretty good Latin scholar, and a citizen so creditable as to be made one of the magistrates of Lichfield ; and, being a man of good sense, and skill in his trade, he acquired a reasonable share of wealth, of which however he afterwards lost the greatest part, by engaging unsuccessfully in a manufacture of parchment. He was a zealous high-church man and royalist, and retained his attachment to the unfortunate house of Stuart, though he reconciled himself, by casuistical arguments of expediency and necessity, to take the oaths imposed by the prevailing power.

6. *Oxford* [1728].

That a man in Mr. Michael Johnson's circumstances should think of sending his son to the expensive University of Oxford, at his own charge, seems very improbable. The subject was too delicate to question Johnson upon : But I have been assured by Dr. Taylor, that the scheme never would have taken place, had not a gentleman of Shropshire, one of his schoolfellows, spontaneously undertaken to support him at Oxford, in the character of his companion; though, in fact, he never received any assistance whatever from that gentleman.

He, however, went to Oxford, and was entered a Commoner of Pembroke College, on the 31st of October, 1728, being then in his nineteenth year.

The Reverend Dr. Adams, who afterwards presided over Pembroke College with universal esteem, told me he was present, and gave me some account of what passed on the night of Johnson's arrival at Oxford. On that evening, his father, who had anxiously accompanied him, found means to have him introduced to Mr. Jorden, who was to be his tutor. . . .

His father seemed very full of the merits of his son, and told the company he was a good scholar, and a poet, and wrote Latin verses. His figure and manner appeared strange to them; but he behaved modestly, and sat silent, till upon something which occurred in the course of conversation, he suddenly struck in and quoted Macrobius; and thus he gave the first impression of that more extensive reading in which he had indulged himself.

7. *Study* [1729].

When I once asked him whether a person whose name I have now forgotten, studied hard, he answered 'No, Sir. I do not believe he studied hard. I never knew a man who studied hard. I conclude, indeed, from the effects, that some men have studied hard, as Bentley and Clarke.' Trying him by that criterion upon which he formed his judgement of others, we may be absolutely certain, both from his writings and his conversation, that his reading was very extensive. Dr. Adam Smith, than whom few were better judges on this subject, once observed to me, that 'Johnson knew more books than any man alive.' He had a peculiar facility in seizing at once what was valuable in any book, without submitting to the labour of perusing it from beginning to end. He had, from the irritability of his constitution, at all times, an impatience and hurry when he either read or wrote. A certain apprehension, arising from novelty, made him write his first exercise at College twice over; but he never took that trouble with any other composition; and we shall see that his most excellent works were struck off at a heat, with rapid exertion[1].

8. *David Garrick* [1731].

'At this man's table I enjoyed many cheerful and instructive hours, with companions, such as are not often found—with one who has lengthened, and one who has gladdened life; with Dr. James, whose skill in physick will be long remembered; and with David Garrick, whom I hoped to have gratified with this character of our common friend. But what are the hopes of man! I am disappointed by that stroke of

---

[1] He told Dr. Burney that he never wrote any of his works that were printed, twice over. Dr. Burney's wonder at seeing several pages of his *Lives of the Poets*, in Manuscript, with scarce a blot or erasure, drew this observation from him. [M.]

death, which has eclipsed the gaiety of nations, and impoverished the publick stock of harmless pleasure.'

9. *Johnson's Private Academy* [1736].

He now set up a private academy, for which purpose he hired a large house, well situated near his native city. In the *Gentleman's Magazine* for 1736, there is the following advertisement:

'At Edial, near Lichfield, in Staffordshire, young gentlemen are boarded and taught the Latin and Greek languages, by SAMUEL JOHNSON.'

But the only pupils that were put under his care were the celebrated David Garrick and his brother George, and a Mr. Offely, a young gentleman of good fortune who died early. As yet, his name had nothing of that celebrity which afterwards commanded the highest attention and respect of mankind. Had such an advertisement appeared after the publication of his *London*, or his *Rambler*, or his *Dictionary*, how would it have burst upon the world! with what eagerness would the great and the wealthy have embraced an opportunity of putting their sons under the learned tuition of SAMUEL JOHNSON.

10. *He goes to London.* [1736].

Johnson now thought of trying his fortune in London, the great field of genius and exertion, where talents of every kind have the fullest scope, and the highest encouragement. It is a memorable circumstance that his pupil David Garrick went thither at the same time[1],

---

[1] Both of them used to talk pleasantly of this their first journey to London. Garrick, evidently meaning to embellish a

with intention to complete his education, and follow the profession of the law, from which he was soon diverted by his decided preference for the stage.

11. *Plain Living* [1737].

He had a little money when he came to town, and he knew how he could live in the cheapest manner. His first lodgings were at the house of Mr. Norris, a staymaker, in Exeter-street, adjoining Catharine-street, in the Strand. ' I dined (said he) very well for eight-pence, with very good company, at the Pine Apple in New-street, just by. Several of them had travelled. They expected to meet every day; but did not know one another's names. It used to cost the rest a shilling, for they drank wine; but I had a cut of meat for six-pence, and bread for a penny, and gave the waiter a penny; so that I was quite well served, nay, better than the rest, for they gave the waiter nothing.' He at this time, I believe, abstained entirely from fermented liquors: a practice to which he rigidly conformed for many years together, at different periods of his life.

12· *The Gentleman's Magazine* [1738].

It appears that he was now enlisted by Mr. Cave as a regular coadjutor in his magazine, by which he

little, said one day in my hearing, 'we rode and tied.' And the Bishop of Killaloe informed me, that at another time, when Johnson and Garrick were dining together in a pretty large company, Johnson humorously ascertaining the chronology of something, expressed himself thus: 'that was the year when I came to London with two-pence half-penny in my pocket.' Garrick overhearing him, exclaimed, 'Eh? what do you say? with two-pence half-penny in your pocket?'—JOHNSON, 'Why yes; when I came with two-pence half-penny in *my* pocket, and thou, Davy, with three half-pence in thine.'

probably obtained a tolerable livelihood. At what
time, or by what means, he had acquired a competent
knowledge both of French and Italian, I do not know;
but he was so well skilled in them, as to be sufficiently
qualified for a translator. That part of his labour which
consisted in emendation and improvement of the pro-
ductions of other contributors, like that employed in
levelling ground, can be perceived only by those who
had an opportunity of comparing the original with the
altered copy. What we certainly know to have been
done by him in this way, was the Debates in both
houses of Parliament, under the name of 'The Senate of
Lilliput', sometimes with feigned denominations of the
several speakers, sometimes with denominations formed
of the letters of their real names, in the manner of
what is called anagram, so that they might easily be
decyphered. Parliament then kept the press in a kind
of mysterious awe, which made it necessary to have
recourse to such devices. In our time it has acquired
an unrestrained freedom, so that the people in all
parts of the kingdom have a fair, open, and exact
report of the actual proceedings of their representatives
and legislators, which in our constitution is highly to
be valued; though, unquestionably, there has of late
been too much reason to complain of the petulance
with which obscure scribblers have presumed to treat
men of the most respectable character and situation.

This important article of the *Gentleman's Magazine* was, for several years, executed by Mr.
William Guthrie. . . . . The debates in Parliament,
which were brought home and digested by Guthrie,

whose memory, though surpassed by others who have since followed him in the same department, was yet very quick and tenacious, were sent by Cave to Johnson for his revision; and, after some time, when Guthrie had attained to greater variety of employment, and the speeches were more and more enriched by the accession of Johnson's genius, it was resolved that he should do the whole himself, from the scanty notes furnished by persons employed to attend in both houses of Parliament. Sometimes, however, as he himself told me, he had nothing more communicated to him than the names of the several speakers, and the part which they had taken in the debate.

Thus was Johnson employed during some of the best years of his life, as a mere literary labourer 'for gain, not glory,' solely to obtain an honest support. He however indulged himself in occasional little sallies, which the French so happily express by the term *jeux d'esprit*, and which will be noticed in their order, in the progress of this work.

13. LONDON, *a Poem; Pope's Admiration* [1739].

As Mr. Pope's note concerning Johnson, alluded to in a former page, refers both to his *London*, and his *Marmor Norfolciense*, I have deferred inserting it till now. I am indebted for it to Dr. Percy, the Bishop of Dromore, who permitted me to copy it from the original in his possession. It was presented to his Lordship by Sir Joshua Reynolds, to whom it was given by the son of Mr. Richardson the painter, the person to whom it is addressed. I have transcribed it with minute exactness, that the peculiar mode of writing, and imperfect spelling of that celebrated poet, may be exhibited to the curious in literature. It justifies Swift's epithet of ' paper-sparing Pope,' for it is written on a slip no larger than a common message-card, and was sent to Mr. Richardson, along with the *Imitation of Juvenal.*

'This is imitated by one Johnson who put in for a Publick-school in Shropshire, but was disappointed. He has an infirmity of the convulsive kind, that attacks him sometimes, so as to make Him a sad Spectacle. Mr. P. from the Merit of This Work which was all the knowledge he had of Him endeavour'd to serve Him without his own application; & wrote to my L^d gore, but he did not succeed. Mr. Johnson published afterw^{ds} another Poem in Latin with Notes the whole very Humerous call'd the Norfolk Prophecy. P.'

14. *The* DICTIONARY [1747].

But the year 1747 is distinguished as the epoch, when Johnson's arduous and important work, his DICTIONARY OF THE ENGLISH LANGUAGE, was announced to the world, by the publication of its Plan or *Prospectus.*

How long this immense undertaking had been the object of his contemplation, I do not know. I once asked him by what means he had attained to that astonishing knowledge of our language, by which he was enabled to realise a design of such extent, and accumulated difficulty. He told me, that ' it was not the effect of particular study; but that it had grown up in his mind insensibly.' I have been informed by Mr. James Dodsley, that several years before this period, when Johnson was one day sitting in his brother Robert's shop, he heard his brother suggest to him, that a Dictionary of the English Language would be a work that would be well received by the publick ; that Johnson seemed at first to catch at the proposition, but, after a pause, said, in his abrupt decisive manner, ' I believe I shall not undertake it.' That he, however, had bestowed much thought upon the subject, before he published his *Plan*, is evident from the enlarged, clear, and accurate views which it exhibits ; and we find him mentioning in that tract, that many of the writers whose testimonies were to be produced as authorities, were selected by Pope ; which proves that he had been furnished, probably by Mr. Robert Dodsley, with whatever hints that eminent poet had contributed towards a great literary project, that had been the subject of important consideration in a former reign.

The booksellers who contracted with Johnson, single and unaided, for the execution of a work, which in other countries has not been effected but by the co-operating exertions of many, were Mr. Robert Dodsley, Mr. Charles Hitch, Mr. Andrew Millar, the two Messieurs Longman, and the two Messieurs Knapton. The price stipulated was fifteen hundred and seventy-five pounds. . . . .

Dr. Adams found him one day busy at his *Dictionary*, when the following dialogue ensued. · ' ADAMS. This is a great work, Sir. How are you to get all the etymologies? JOHNSON. Why, Sir, here is a shelf with Junius, and Skinner, and others ; and there is a Welch gentleman who has published a collection of Welch proverbs,

who will help me with the Welch. ADAMS. But, Sir, how
can you do this in three years? JOHNSON, Sir, I have
no doubt that I can do it in three years. ADAMS. But
the French Academy, which consists of forty members,
took forty years to compile their Dictionary. JOHNSON.
Sir, thus it is. This is the proportion. Let me see;
forty times forty is sixteen hundred. As three to sixteen hundred, so is the proportion of an Englishman
to a Frenchman.' With so much ease and pleasantry
could he talk of that prodigious labour which he had
undertaken to execute.

15. *Death of his Wife* [1752].

The next day he wrote as follows:

'TO THE REVEREND DR. TAYLOR.

'DEAR SIR,—Let me have your company and instruction. Do not live away from me. My distress is great.

'Pray desire Mrs. Taylor to inform me what mourn-
ing I should buy for my mother and Miss Porter, and
bring a note in writing with you.

'Remember me in your prayers, for vain is the help
of man. I am, dear Sir, &c.

'March 18, 1752.'   'SAM. JOHNSON.'

16. *Bennet Langton and Topham Beauclerk* [1752].

His acquaintance with Bennet Langton, Esq. of
Langton, in Lincolnshire, another much valued friend,
commenced soon after the conclusion of his *Rambler*;
which that gentleman, then a youth, had read with so
much admiration, that he came to London chiefly with

the view of endeavouring to be introduced to its authour. . . . .

Mr. Langton afterwards went to pursue his studies at Trinity College, Oxford, where he formed an acquaintance with his fellow student, Mr. Topham Beauclerk; who, though their opinions and modes of life were so different, that it seemed utterly improbable that they should at all agree, had so ardent a love of literature, so acute an understanding, such elegance of manners, and so well discerned the excellent qualities of Mr. Langton, a gentleman eminent not only for worth and learning, but for an inexhaustible fund of entertaining conversation, that they became intimate friends.

Johnson, soon after this acquaintance began, passed a considerable time at Oxford. He at first thought it strange that Langton should associate so much with one who had the character of being loose, both in his principles and practice; but, by degrees, he himself was fascinated. Mr. Beauclerk's being of the St. Alban's family, and having, in some particulars, a resemblance to Charles the Second, contributed, in Johnson's imagination, to throw a lustre upon his other qualities; and, in a short time, the moral, pious Johnson, and the gay, dissipated Beauclerk, were companions. 'What a coalition! (said Garrick, when he heard of this;) I shall have my old friend to bail out of the Round-house.' But I can bear testimony that it was a very agreeable association. Beauclerk was too polite, and valued learning and wit too much, to offend Johnson by sallies of infidelity or licentiousness; and Johnson delighted in the good qualities of Beauclerk, and hoped to correct the evil. Innumerable were the scenes in which Johnson was amused by these young men. Beauclerk could take more liberty with him, than any body with whom I ever saw him; but, on the other hand, Beauclerk was not spared by his respectable companion, when reproof was proper. Beauclerk had such a propensity to satire, that at one time Johnson said to him, 'You never open your mouth but with intention to give pain; and you have often given me pain, not from the power of what you said, but from seeing your intention.' At another time applying to him, with a slight alteration, a line of Pope, he said,

'Thy love of folly, and thy scorn of fools—

Every thing thou dost shews the one, and every thing thou say'st the other.' At another time he said to him, 'Thy body is all vice, and thy mind all virtue.' Beauclerk not seeming to relish the compliment, Johnson said, 'Nay, Sir, Alexander the Great, marching in triumph into Babylon, could not have desired to have had more said to him.'

***   17. *Letter to Lord Chesterfield* [1754].
Lord Chesterfield, to whom Johnson had paid the high compliment of addressing to his Lordship the *Plan* of his *Dictionary*, had behaved to him in such a manner as to excite his contempt and indignation. . . . . He told me, that there never was any particular incident which produced a quarrel between Lord Chesterfield and him; but that his Lordship's

continued neglect was the reason why he resolved
to have no connection with him. When the *Dictionary* was upon the eve of publication, Lord Chesterfield, who, it is said, had flattered himself with expectations that Johnson would dedicate the work to him,
attempted in a courtly manner, to sooth, and insinuate
himself with the Sage, conscious, as it should seem, of
the cold indifference with which he had treated its
learned authour; and further attempted to conciliate
him, by writing two papers in *The World*, in recommendation of the work; and it must be confessed, that
they contain some studied compliments, so finely
turned, that if there had been no previous offence, it
is probable that Johnson would have been highly
delighted. Praise, in general, was pleasing to him;
but by praise from a man of rank and elegant accomplishments, he was peculiarly gratified. . . . .

This courtly device failed of its effect. Johnson,
who thought that 'all was false and hollow,' despised
the honeyed words, and was even indignant that Lord
Chesterfield should, for a moment, imagine that he
could be the dupe of such an artifice. His expression
to me concerning Lord Chesterfield, upon this occasion,
was, 'Sir, after making great professions, he had, for
many years, taken no notice of me; but when my
Dictionary was coming out, he fell a scribbling in
The World about it. Upon which, I wrote him a
letter expressed in civil terms, but such as might shew
him that I did not mind what he said or wrote, and
that I had done with him.'

This is that celebrated letter of which so much has

been said, and about which curiosity has been so long excited, without being gratified. I for many years solicited Johnson to favour me with a copy of it, that so excellent a composition might not be lost to posterity. He delayed from time to time to give it me ; till at last in 1781, when we were on a visit at Mr. Dilly's, at Southill in Bedfordshire, he was pleased to dictate it to me from memory. He afterwards found among his papers a copy of it, which he had dictated to Mr. Baretti, with its title and corrections, in his own handwriting. This he gave to Mr. Langton ; adding that if it were to come into print, he wished it to be from that copy. By Mr. Langton's kindness, I am enabled to enrich my work with a perfect transcript of what the world has so eagerly desired to see.

'TO THE RIGHT HONOURABLE THE EARL OF CHESTERFIELD.

'MY LORD,   February 7, 1755.

'I have been lately informed, by the proprietor of *The World*, that two papers, in which my Dictionary is recommended to the publick, were written by your Lordship. To be so distinguished, is an honour, which, being very little accustomed to favours from the great, I know not well how to receive, or in what terms to acknowledge.

'When, upon some slight encouragement, I first visited your Lordship, I was overpowered, like the rest of mankind, by the enchantment of your address ; and could not forbear to wish that I might boast myself *Le vainqueur du vainqueur de la terre* ;—

that I might obtain that regard for which I saw the world contending; but I found my attendance so little encouraged, that neither pride nor modesty would suffer me to continue it. When I had once addressed your Lordship in publick, I had exhausted all the art of pleasing which a retired and uncourtly scholar can possess. I had done all that I could; and no man is well pleased to have his all neglected, be it ever so little.

'Seven years, my Lord, have now past, since I waited in your outward rooms, or was repulsed from your door; during which time I have been pushing on my work through difficulties, of which it is useless to complain, and have brought it, at last, to the verge of publication, without one act of assistance[1], one word of encouragement, or one smile of favour. Such treatment I did not expect, for I never had a Patron before.

'The shepherd in Virgil grew at last acquainted with Love, and found him a native of the rocks.

'Is not a Patron, my Lord, one who looks with unconcern on a man struggling for life in the water, and, when he has reached ground, encumbers him with help? The notice which you have been pleased to take of my labours, had it been early, had been

---

[1] The following note is subjoined by Mr. Langton:—'Dr. Johnson, when he gave me this copy of his letter, desired that I would annex to it his information to me, that whereas it is said in the letter that "no assistance has been received," he did once receive from Lord Chesterfield the sum of ten pounds; but as that was so inconsiderable a sum, he thought the mention of it could not properly find place in a letter of the kind that this was.'

kind; but it has been delayed till I am indifferent,
and cannot enjoy it; till I am solitary, and cannot
impart it[1]; till I am known, and do not want it.
I hope it is no very cynical asperity not to confess
obligations where no benefit has been received, or
to be unwilling that the Publick should consider me
as owing that to a Patron, which Providence has
enabled me to do for myself.

'Having carried on my work thus far with so little
obligation to any favourer of learning, I shall not
be disappointed though I should conclude it, if less
be possible, with less; for I have been long wakened
from that dream of hope, in which I once boasted
myself with so much exultation, my Lord, your Lordship's most humble, most obedient servant,

'SAM. JOHNSON.'

18. *The Dictionary Published* [1755]

The *Dictionary*, with a *Grammar and History of
the English Language*, being now at length published,
in two volumes folio, the world contemplated with
wonder so stupendous a work atchieved by one man,
while other countries had thought such undertakings
fit only for whole academies. . . . .

[1] In this passage Dr. Johnson evidently alludes to the loss of
his wife. We find the same tender recollection recurring to his
mind upon innumerable occasions : and, perhaps no man ever
more forcibly felt the truth of the sentiment so elegantly expressed
by my friend Mr. Malone, in his Prologue to Mr. Jephson's
tragedy of JULIA :

'Vain—wealth, and fame, and fortune's fostering care,
If no fond breast the splendid blessings share ;
And, each day's bustling pageantry once past,
There, only there, our bliss is found at last.'

The extensive reading which was absolutely necessary for the accumulation of authorities, and which alone may account for Johnson's retentive mind being enriched with a very large and various store of knowledge and imagery, must have occupied several years. The Preface furnishes an eminent instance of a double talent, of which Johnson was fully conscious. Sir Joshua Reynolds heard him say, ' There are two things which I am confident I can do very well: one is an introduction to any literary work, stating what it is to contain, and how it should be executed in the most perfect manner; the other is a conclusion, shewing from various causes why the execution has not been equal to what the authour promised to himself and to the publick.' . . . .

His introducing his own opinions, and even pre-judices, under general definitions of words, while at the same time the original meaning of the words is not explained, as his *Tory, Whig, Pension, Oats, Excise*, and a few more, cannot be fully defended, and must be placed to the account of capricious and humorous indulgence. . . . .

Let it, however, be remembered, that this indulgence does not display itself only in sarcasm towards others, but sometimes in playful allusion to the notions commonly entertained of his own laborious task. Thus: ' *Grub-street*, the name of a street in London, much inhabited by writers of small histories, *diction-aries*, and temporary poems; whence any mean production is called *Grub-street.*'—' *Lexicographer*, a writer of dictionaries, a *harmless drudge.*' . . . .

He had spent, during the progress of the work, the money for which he had contracted to write his *Dictionary*. We have seen that the reward of his labour was only fifteen hundred and seventy-five pounds; and when the expence of amanuenses and paper, and other articles are deducted, his clear profit was very inconsiderable. I once said to him, 'I am sorry, Sir, you did not get more for your *Dictionary*.' His answer was, 'I am sorry, too. But it was very well. The booksellers are generous liberal-minded men.' He, upon all occasions, did ample justice to their character in this respect. He considered them as the patrons of literature; and, indeed, although they have eventually been considerable gainers by his *Dictionary*, it is to them that we owe its having been undertaken and carried through at the risk of great expence, for they were not absolutely sure of being indemnified.

19. *Defence of Tea* [1756].

His defence of tea against Mr. Jonas Hanway's violent attack upon that elegant and popular beverage, shews how very well a man of genius can write upon the slightest subject, when he writes, as the Italians say, *con amore*: I suppose no person ever enjoyed with more relish the infusion of that fragrant leaf than Johnson. The quantities which he drank of it at all hours were so great, that his nerves must have been uncommonly strong, not to have been extremely relaxed by such an intemperate use of it. He assured me, that he never felt the least inconvenience from it; which is a proof that the fault of his constitution was rather a too great tension of fibres, than the contrary.

20. *Dedication to the Earl of Rochford of Mr. William Payne's* Introduction to the Game of Draughts [1756].

'Triflers may find or make any thing a trifle; but since it is the great characteristick of a wise man to see events in their courses, to obviate consequences, and ascertain contingencies, your Lordship will think nothing a trifle by which the mind is inured to caution, foresight, and circumspection.'

21. *The Irish Language* [1757].

By the favour of Mr. Joseph Cooper Walker, of the Treasury, Dublin, I have obtained a copy of the following letter from Johnson to the venerable authour of *Dissertations on the History of Ireland.*

'To CHARLES O'CONNOR, ESQ.

'SIR,—I have lately, by the favour of Mr. Faulkner, seen your account of Ireland, and cannot forbear to solicit a prosecution of your design. Sir William Temple complains that Ireland is less known than any other country, as to its ancient state. The natives have had little leisure, and little encouragement for enquiry; and strangers, not knowing the language, have had no ability.

'I have long wished that the Irish literature were cultivated. Ireland is known by tradition to have been once the seat of piety and learning; and surely it would be very acceptable to all those who are curious either in the original of nations, or the affinities of languages, to be further informed of the revolution of a people so ancient, and once so illustrious.

'What relation there is between the Welch and Irish language, or between the language of Ireland and that of Biscay, deserves enquiry. Of these provincial and unextended tongues, it seldom happens that more than one are understood by any one man; and, therefore, it seldom happens that a fair comparison can be made. I hope you will continue to cultivate this kind of learning, which has too long lain neglected, and which, if it be suffered to remain in oblivion for another century, may, perhaps, never be retrieved. As I wish well to all useful undertakings, I would not forbear to let you know how much you deserve in my opinion, from all lovers of study, and how much pleasure your work has given to, Sir, your most obliged, and most humble servant,

'London, April 9, 1757.'   'SAM. JOHNSON.'

22. *Shakespeare.*

[1757. *From a letter to Burney.*] 'I am ashamed to tell you that my *Shakspeare* will not be out so soon as I promised my subscribers; but I did not promise them more than I promised myself. It will, however, be published before summer.

'I have sent you a bundle of proposals, which, I think, do not profess more than I have hitherto performed. I have printed many of the plays, and have hitherto left very few passages unexplained; where I am quite at a loss, I confess my ignorance, which is seldom done by commentators.'

[*Communicated by Burney.*] ' " But, Sir, (said Mr. Burney,) you'll have Warburton upon your bones, won't you?" "No, Sir; he'll not come out: he'll only growl in his den." " But you think, Sir, that Warburton is a superiour critick to Theobald?" "O, Sir, he'd make two-and-fifty Theobalds, cut into slices! The worst of Warburton is, that he has a rage for saying something, when there's nothing to be said." '

[1758. *From a letter to Thomas Warton.*] 'DEAR SIR,—Your notes upon my poet were very acceptable. I beg that you will be so kind as to continue your searches. It will be reputable to my work, and suitable to your professorship, to have something of yours in the notes. As you have given no directions about your name, I shall therefore put it. I wish your brother would take the same trouble. A commentary must arise from the fortuitous discoveries of many men in devious walks of literature.'

23. *Death of his Mother* [1759].

TO MISS PORTER IN LICHFIELD.

'You will conceive my sorrow for the loss of my mother, of the best mother. If she were to live again surely I should behave better to her. But she is happy, and what is past is nothing to her; and for me, since I cannot repair my faults to her, I hope repentance will efface them. I return you and all those that have been good to her my sincerest thanks, and pray God to repay you all with infinite advantage. Write to

me, and comfort me, dear child.   I shall be glad likewise, if Kitty will write to me.   I shall send a bill of
twenty pounds in a few days, which I thought to have
brought to my mother; but God suffered it not.   I
have not power or composure to say much more.   God
bless you, and bless us all.

'I am, dear Miss,

'Your affectionate humble servant,

'Jan. 23, 1759.'   'SAM. JOHNSON.'

24.   *The Pension* [1762].

The accession of George the Third to the throne of
these kingdoms, opened a new and brighter prospect
to men of literary merit, who had been honoured with
no mark of royal favour in the preceding reign.   His
present Majesty's education in this country, as well as
his taste and beneficence, prompted him to be the
patron of science and the arts; and early this year
Johnson having been represented to him as a very
learned and good man, without any certain provision,
his Majesty was pleased to grant him a pension of
three hundred pounds a year. . . . . .

'TO THE RIGHT HONOURABLE THE EARL OF BUTE.

'MY LORD,—When the bills were yesterday delivered
to me by Mr. Wedderburne, I was informed by him
of the future favours which his Majesty has, by your
Lordship's recommendation, been induced to intend
for me.

'Bounty always receives part of its value from the
manner in which it is bestowed; your Lordship's

kindness includes every circumstance that can gratify delicacy, or enforce obligation. You have conferred your favours on a man who has neither alliance nor interest, who has not merited them by services, nor courted them by officiousness; you have spared him the shame of solicitation, and the anxiety of suspense.

'What has been thus elegantly given, will, I hope, not be reproachfully enjoyed; I shall endeavour to give your Lordship the only recompense which generosity desires,—the gratification of finding that your benefits are not improperly bestowed. I am, my Lord, your Lordship's most obliged, most obedient, and most humble servant,

'July 20, 1762'   'SAM. JOHNSON.'

25. *Boswell meets Johnson* [1763].

Mr. Thomas Davies the actor, who then kept a bookseller's shop in Russel-street, Covent-garden, told me that Johnson was very much his friend, and came frequently to his house, where he more than once invited me to meet him; but by some unlucky accident or other he was prevented from coming to us. . . . .

At last, on Monday the 16th of May, when I was sitting in Mr. Davies's back-parlour, after having drunk tea with him and Mrs. Davies, Johnson unexpectedly came into the shop; and Mr. Davies having perceived him through the glass-door in the room in which we were sitting, advancing towards us,—he announced his aweful approach to me, somewhat in the manner of an actor in the part of Horatio, when he addresses Hamlet on the appearance of his father's ghost, 'Look, my

Lord, it comes.'   I found that I had a very perfect idea
of Johnson's figure, from the portrait of him painted
by Sir Joshua. Reynolds soon after he had published
his *Dictionary*, in the attitude of sitting in his easy
chair in deep meditation, which was the first picture
his friend did for him, which Sir Joshua very kindly
presented to me, and from which an engraving has
been made for this work.   Mr. Davies mentioned my
name, and respectfully introduced me to him.   I was
much agitated; and recollecting his prejudice against
the Scotch, of which I had heard much, I said to Davies,
'Don't tell where I come from.'—'From Scotland,'
cried Davies roguishly.   'Mr. Johnson, (said I) I do
indeed come from Scotland, but I cannot help it.'   I
am willing to flatter myself that I meant this as light
pleasantry to sooth and conciliate him, and not as an
humiliating abasement at the expence of my country.
But however that might be, this speech was somewhat
unlucky; for with that quickness of wit for which he
was so remarkable, he seized the expression 'come
from Scotland,' which I used in the sense of being of
that country; and, as if I had said that I had come away
from it, or left it, retorted, 'That, Sir, I find, is what
a very great many of your countrymen cannot help.'
This stroke stunned me a good deal; and when we
had sat down, I felt myself not a little embarrassed, and
apprehensive of what might come next.   He then
addressed himself to Davies: 'What do you think of
Garrick? He has refused me an order for the play for
Miss Williams, because he knows the house will be
full, and that an order would be worth three shillings.

Eager to take any opening to get into conversation with him, I ventured to say, 'O, Sir, I cannot think Mr. Garrick would grudge such a trifle to you.' 'Sir, (said he, with a stern look,) I have known David Garrick longer than you have done: and I know no right you have to talk to me on the subject.' Perhaps I deserved this check; for it was rather presumptuous in me, an entire stranger, to express any doubt of the justice of his animadversion upon his old acquaintance and pupil. I now felt myself much mortified, and began to think that the hope which I had long indulged of obtaining his acquaintance was blasted. And, in truth, had not my ardour been uncommonly strong, and my resolution uncommonly persevering, so rough a reception might have deterred me for ever from making any further attempts. Fortunately, however, I remained upon the field not wholly discomfited; and was soon rewarded by hearing some of his conversation. . . .

I was highly pleased with the extraordinary vigour of his conversation, and regretted that I was drawn away from it by an engagement at another place. I had, for a part of the evening, been left alone with him, and had ventured to make an observation now and then, which he received very civilly; so that I was satisfied that though there was a roughness in his manner, there was no ill-nature in his disposition. Davies followed me to the door, and when I complained to him a little of the hard blows which the great man had given me, he kindly took upon him to console me by saying, 'Don't be uneasy. I can see he likes you very well.'

26. *Kit Smart* [1763].

Concerning this unfortunate poet, Christopher Smart, who was confined in a mad-house, he had, at another time, the following conversation with Dr. Burney:—BURNEY. 'How does poor Smart do, Sir; is he likely to recover?' JOHNSON. 'It seems as if his mind had ceased to struggle with the disease; for he grows fat upon it.' BURNEY. 'Perhaps, Sir, that may be from want of exercise.' JOHNSON. 'No, Sir; he has partly as much exercise as he used to have, for he digs in the garden. Indeed, before his confinement, he used for exercise to walk to the ale-house; but he was *carried* back again. I did not think he ought to be shut up. His infirmities were not noxious to society. He insisted on people praying with him; and I'd as lief pray with Kit Smart as any one else. Another charge was, that he did not love clean linen; and I have no passion for it.'

27. *Late Hours* [1763].

When I rose a second time he again pressed me to stay, which I did.

He told me, that he generally went abroad at four in the afternoon, and seldom came home till two in the morning. I took the liberty to ask if he did not think it wrong to live thus, and not make more use of his great talents. He owned it was a bad habit. On reviewing, at the distance of many years, my journal of this period, I wonder how, at my first visit, I ventured to talk to him so freely, and that he bore it with so much indulgence.

28. *Religion* [1763].

I acknowledged, that though educated very strictly
in the principles of religion, I had for some time been
misled into a certain degree of infidelity; but that I
was come now to a better way of thinking, and was
fully satisfied of the truth of the Christian revelation,
though I was not clear as to every point considered
to be orthodox.   Being at all times a curious examiner
of the human mind, and pleased with an undisguised
display of what had passed in it, he called to me with
warmth, 'Give me your hand; I have taken a liking
to you.'   He then began to descant upon the force of
testimony, and the little we could know of final causes;
so that the objections of, why was it so? or why was
it not so? ought not to disturb us: adding, that he
himself had at one period been guilty of a temporary
neglect of religion, but that it was not the result of
argument, but mere absence of thought.

29. *Critical Strictures* [1763].

I mentioned Mallet's tragedy of *Elvira*, which had
been acted the preceding winter at Drury-lane, and
that the Honourable Andrew Erskine, Mr. Dempster,
and myself, had joined in writing a pamphlet, entitled,
Critical Strictures against it.   That the mildness of
Dempster's disposition had, however, relented; and he
had candidly said, 'We have hardly a right to abuse
this tragedy: for bad as it is, how vain should either
of us be to write one not near so good.'   JOHNSON. 'Why
no, Sir; this is not just reasoning.   You *may* abuse a

tragedy, though you cannot write one. You may scold a carpenter who has made you a bad table, though you cannot make a table. It is not your trade to make tables.'

30. *Oliver Goldsmith* [1763].

As Dr. Oliver Goldsmith will frequently appear in this narrative, I shall endeavour to make my readers in some degree acquainted with his singular character. He was a native of Ireland, and a contemporary with Mr. Burke, at Trinity College, Dublin, but did not then give much promise of future celebrity. He, however, observed to Mr. Malone, that 'though he made no great figure in mathematicks, which was a study in much repute there, he could turn an Ode of Horace into English better than any of them.' He afterwards studied physick at Edinburgh, and upon the Continent; and I have been informed, was enabled to pursue his travels on foot, partly by demanding at Universities to enter the lists as a disputant, by which, according to the custom of many of them, he was entitled to the premium of a crown, when luckily for him his challenge was not accepted; so that, as I once observed to Dr. Johnson, he *disputed* his passage through Europe. He then came to England, and was employed successively in the capacities of an usher to an academy, a corrector of the press, a reviewer, and a writer for a news-paper. He had sagacity enough to cultivate assiduously the acquaintance of Johnson, and his faculties were gradually enlarged by the contemplation of such a model. To me and many others it appeared that he studiously copied the manner of Johnson, though, indeed, upon a smaller scale.

At this time I think he had published nothing with his name, though it was pretty generally known that *one Dr. Goldsmith* was the authour of *An Enquiry into the present State of polite Learning in Europe*, and of *The Citizen of the World*, a series of letters supposed to be written from London by a Chinese. No man had the art of displaying with more advantage as a writer, whatever literary acquisitions he made. ' *Nihil quod tetigit non ornavit* [1].' His mind resembled a fertile, but thin soil. There was a quick, but not a strong vegetation, of whatever chanced to be thrown upon it. No deep root could be struck. The oak of the forest did not grow there; but the elegant shrubbery and the fragrant parterre appeared in gay succession. It had been generally circulated and believed that he was a mere fool in conversation; but, in truth, this has been greatly exaggerated. He had, no doubt, a more than common share of that hurry of ideas which we often find in his countrymen, and which sometimes produces a laughable confusion in expressing them. He was very much what the French call *un étourdi*, and from vanity and an eager desire of being conspicuous wherever he was, he frequently talked carelessly without knowledge of the subject, or even without thought. His person was short, his countenance coarse and vulgar, his deportment that of a scholar aukwardly affecting the easy gentleman.

[1] See his Epitaph in Westminster Abbey, written by Dr. Johnson.

31. *The Vicar of Wakefield* [1763].

Mrs. Piozzi and Sir John Hawkins have strangely mis-stated the history of Goldsmith's situation and Johnson's friendly interference, when this novel was sold. I shall give it authentically from Johnson's own exact narration: 'I received one morning a message from poor Goldsmith that he was in great distress, and as it was not in his power to come to me, begging that I would come to him as soon as possible. I sent him a guinea, and promised to come to him directly. I accordingly went as soon as I was drest, and found that his landlady had arrested him for his rent, at which he was in a violent passion. I perceived that he had already changed my guinea, and had got a bottle of Madeira and a glass before him. I put the cork into the bottle, desired he would be calm, and began to talk to him of the means by which he might be extricated. He then told me that he had a novel ready for the press, which he produced to me. I looked into it, and saw its merit; told the landlady I should soon return, and having gone to a bookseller, sold it for sixty pounds. I brought Goldsmith the money, and he discharged his rent, not without rating his landlady in a high tone for having used him so ill.'

32. *Boswell's Method* [1763].

Let me here apologize for the imperfect manner in which I am obliged to exhibit Johnson's conversation at this period. In the early part of my acquaintance with him, I was so wrapt in admiration of his extraordinary colloquial talents, and so little accustomed to his peculiar mode of expression, that I found it extremely difficult to recollect and record his conversation with its genuine vigour and vivacity. In progress of time, when my mind was, as it were, *strongly impregnated with the Johnsonian æther*, I could, with much more facility and exactness, carry in my memory and commit to paper the exuberant variety of his wisdom and wit.

33. *Rhyme* [1763].

He enlarged very convincingly upon the excellence of rhyme over blank verse in English poetry. I mentioned to him that Dr. Adam Smith, in his lectures upon composition, when I studied under him in the College of Glasgow, had maintained the same opinion strenuously, and I repeated some of his arguments. JOHNSON. 'Sir, I was once in company with Smith, and we did not take to each other; but had I known that he loved rhyme as much as you tell me he does, I should have HUGGED him.'

34. *Let us Count our Spoons* [1763].

I described to him an impudent fellow from Scotland, who affected to be a savage, and railed at all established systems. JOHNSON. 'There is nothing surprizing in this, Sir. He wants to make himself conspicuous. He would tumble in a hogstye, as long as you looked at him and called to him to come out. But let him alone, never mind him, and he'll soon give it over.'

I added, that the same person maintained that there was no distinction between virtue and vice. JOHNSON. 'Why, Sir, if the fellow does not think as he speaks, he is lying; and I see not what honour he can propose to himself from having the character of a lyar. But if he does really think that there is no distinction between virtue and vice, why, Sir, when he leaves our houses let us count our spoons.'

35. *Charles the Second* [1763].

It was suggested that Kings must be unhappy, because they are deprived of the greatest of all satisfactions, easy and unreserved society. JOHNSON. 'That is an ill-founded notion. Being a King does not exclude a man from such society. Great Kings have always been social. The King of Prussia, the only great King at present, is very social. Charles the Second, the last King of England who was a man of parts, was social; and our Henrys and Edwards were all social.'

36. *The Virtues of the Young* [1763].

At night, Mr. Johnson and I supped in a private room at the Turk's Head coffee-house, in the Strand. 'I encourage this house (said he;) for the mistress of it is a good civil woman, and has not much business.'

'Sir, I love the acquaintance of young people; because, in the first place, I don't like to think myself growing old. In the next place, young acquaintances must last longest, if they do last; and then, Sir, young men have more virtue than old men; they

have more generous sentiments in every respect.
I love the young dogs of this age: they have more
wit and humour and knowledge of life than we had;
but then the dogs are not so good scholars. Sir, in
my early years I read very hard. It is a sad reflection,
but a true one, that I knew almost as much at eigh-
teen as I do now. My judgement, to be sure, was not
so good; but I had all the facts. I remember very
well, when I was at Oxford, an old gentleman said to
me, " Young man, ply your book diligently now, and
acquire a stock of knowledge; for when years come
upon you, you will find that poring upon books will
be but an irksome task." '

37. *The Western Islands* [1763].

The mention of this gentleman led us to talk of
the Western Islands of Scotland, to visit which he
expressed a wish that then appeared to me a very
romantick fancy, which I little thought would be afterwards realised. He told me, that his father had put
Martin's account of those islands into his hands when
he was very young, and that he was highly pleased
with it; that he was particularly struck with the St.
Kilda man's notion that the high church of Glasgow
had been hollowed out of a rock; a circumstance to
which old Mr. Johnson had directed his attention.
He said, he would go to the Hebrides with me, when
I returned from my travels, unless some very good
companion should offer when I was absent, which he
did not think probable; adding, ' There are few people
to whom I take so much to as you.' And when I

talked of my leaving England, he said with a very
affectionate air, ' My dear Boswell, I should be very
unhappy at parting, did I think we were not to meet
again.' I cannot too often remind my readers, that
although such instances of his kindness are doubtless
very. flattering to me, yet I hope my recording them
will be ascribed to a better motive than to vanity ;
for they afford unquestionable evidence of his tenderness and complacency, which some, while they were
forced to acknowledge his great powers, have been so
strenuous to deny.

38. *Education of Children* [1763].

We talked of the education of children ; and I asked
him what he thought was best to teach them first.
JOHNSON. ' Sir, it is no matter what you teach them
first, any more than what leg you shall put into your
breeches first. Sir, you may stand disputing which is
best to put in first, but in the mean time your breech
is bare. Sir, while your are considering which of two
things you should teach your child first, another boy
has learnt them both.'

39. *Thomas Sheridan* [1763].

He laughed heartily, when I mentioned to him a
saying of his concerning Mr. Thomas Sheridan, which
Foote took a wicked pleasure to circulate. ' Why,
Sir, Sherry is dull, naturally dull; but it must have
taken him a great deal of pains to become what we
now see him. Such an excess of stupidity, Sir, is
not in Nature.' ' So (said he,) I allowed him all his
own merit.'

40. *Boswell's Method* [1763].

We staid so long at Greenwich, that our sail up the river, in our return to London, was by no means so pleasant as in the morning; for the night air was so cold that it made me shiver. I was the more sensible of it from having sat up all the night before, recollecting and writing in my journal what I thought worthy of preservation ; an exertion, which, during the first part of my acquaintance with Johnson, I frequently made. I remember having sat up four nights in one week, without being much incommoded in the day time.

41. *A Woman's Preaching* [1763].

Next day, Sunday, July 31, I told him I had been that morning at a meeting of the people called Quakers, where I had heard a woman preach. JOHNSON. ' Sir, a woman's preaching is like a dog's walking on his hinder legs. It is not done well; but you are surprized to find it done at all.'

42. *Boswell sets out on his Travels* [1763].

On Friday, August 5, we set out early in the morning in the Harwich stage coach. A fat elderly gentlewoman, and a young Dutchman, seemed the most inclined among us to conversation. At the inn where we dined, the gentlewoman said that she had done her best to educate her children ; and particularly, that she had never suffered them to be a moment idle. JOHNSON. ' I wish, Madam, you would educate me too ; for I have been an idle fellow all my life.' ' I am sure, Sir, (said

she) you have not been idle.' JOHNSON. 'Nay,
Madam, it is very true; and that gentleman there
(pointing to me,) has been idle. He was idle at
Edinburgh. His father sent him to Glasgow, where
he continued to be idle. He then came to London,
where he has been very idle; and now he is going to
Utrecht, where he will be as idle as ever.' I asked
him privately how he could expose me so. JOHNSON.
'Poh, poh! (said he) they knew nothing about you,
and will think of it no more.' ·

✗✱ 43. *Boswell at Utrecht* [1763].

Utrecht seeming at first very dull to me, after the
animated scenes of London, my spirits were grievously
affected; and I wrote to Johnson a plaintive and des-
ponding letter, to which he paid no regard. Afterwards, when I had acquired a firmer tone of mind, I
wrote him a second letter, expressing much anxiety to
hear from him. At length I received the following
epistle, which was of important service to me, and, I
trust, will be so to many others.

A Mr. Mr. BOSWELL, *à la Cour de l'Empereur,*
Utrecht.

'DEAR SIR,—You are not to think yourself forgotten,
or criminally neglected, that you have had yet no letter
from me. I love to see my friends, to hear from them,
to talk to them, and to talk of them; but it is not
without a considerable effort of resolution that I prevail
upon myself to write. I would not, however, gratify
my own indolence by the omission of any important
duty, or any office of real kindness.

'To tell you that I am or am not well, that I have or have not been in the country, that I drank your health in the room in which we sat last together, and that your acquaintance continue to speak of you with their former kindness, topicks with which those letters are commonly filled which are written only for the sake of writing, I seldom shall think worth communicating; but if I can have it in my power to calm any harassing disquiet, to excite any virtuous desire, to rectify any important opinion, or fortify any generous resolution, you need not doubt but I shall at least wish to prefer the pleasure of gratifying a friend much less esteemed than yourself, before the gloomy calm of idle vacancy. Whether I shall easily arrive at an exact punctuality of correspondence, I cannot tell. I shall, at present, expect that you will receive this in return for two which I have had from you. The first, indeed, gave me an account so hopeless of the state of your mind, that it hardly admitted or deserved an answer; by the second I was much better pleased: and the pleasure will still be increased by such a narrative of the progress of your studies, as may evince the continuance of an equal and rational application of your mind to some useful enquiry.

'You will, perhaps, wish to ask, what study I would recommend. I shall not speak of theology, because it ought not to be considered as a question whether you shall endeavour to know the will of GOD.

'I shall, therefore, consider only such studies as we are at liberty to pursue or to neglect; and of these I know not how you will make a better choice, than by studying the civil law, as your father advises, and the ancient languages, as you had determined for yourself; at least resolve, while you remain in any settled residence, to spend a certain number of hours every day amongst your books. The dissipation of thought, of which you complain, is nothing more than the vacillation of a mind suspended between different motives, and changing its direction as any motive gains or loses strength. If you can but kindle in your mind any strong desire, if you can but keep predominant any wish for some particular excellence or attainment, the gusts of imagination will break away, without any effect upon your conduct, and commonly without any traces left upon the memory.

'There lurks, perhaps, in every human heart a desire of distinction, which inclines every man first to hope, and then to believe, that Nature has given him something peculiar to himself. This vanity makes one mind nurse aversion, and another actuate desires, till they rise by art much above their original state of power; and as affectation, in time, improves to habit, they at last tyrannise over him who at first encouraged them only for show. Every desire is a viper in the bosom, who, while he was chill, was harmless; but when warmth gave him strength, exerted it in poison. You know a gentleman, who, when first he set his foot in the gay world, as he prepared himself to whirl in the vortex of pleasure, imagined a total indifference and universal negligence to be the most agreeable concomitants of youth, and the strongest indication of an airy temper and a quick apprehension. Vacant to

every object, and sensible of every impulse, he thought
that all appearance of diligence would deduct something
from the reputation of genius; and hoped that he
should appear to attain, amidst all the ease of careless-
ness, and all the tumult of diversion, that knowledge
and those accomplishments which mortals of the
common fabrick obtain only by mute abstraction and
solitary drudgery.   He tried this scheme of life awhile,
was made weary of it by his sense and his virtue; he
then wished to return to his studies; and finding long
habits of idleness and pleasure harder to be cured than
he expected, still willing to retain his claim to some
extraordinary prerogatives, resolved the common
consequences of irregularity into an unalterable decree
of destiny, and concluded that Nature had originally
formed him incapable of rational employment.

'Let all such fancies, illusive and destructive, be banish-
ed henceforward from your thoughts for ever.   Resolve,
and keep your resolution; choose, and pursue your
choice. If you spend this day in study, you will find
yourself still more able to study to-morrow; not that you
are to expect that you shall at once obtain a complete
victory. Depravity is not very easily overcome. Resolution will sometimes relax, and diligence will sometimes
be interrupted; but let no accidental surprize or devia-
tion, whether short or long, dispose you to despondency.
Consider these failings as incident to all mankind.
Begin again where you left off, and endeavour to avoid
the seducements that prevailed over you before.

'This, my dear Boswell, is advice which, perhaps,
has been often given you, and given you without effect.

But this advice, if you will not take from others, you must take from your own reflections, if you purpose to do the duties of the station to which the bounty of Providence has called you.

' Let me have a long letter from you as soon as you can. I hope you continue your journal, and enrich it with many observations upon the country in which you reside. It will be a favour if you can get me any books in the Frisick language, and can enquire how the poor are maintained in the Seven Provinces. I am, dear Sir, your most affectionate servant,

'London, Dec. 8, 1763.'   'SAM. JOHNSON.'

44. *The Club* [1764].

Soon after his return to London, which was in February, was founded that CLUB which existed long without a name, but at Mr. Garrick's funeral became distinguished by the title of THE LITERARY CLUB. Sir Joshua Reynolds had the merit of being the first proposer of it, to which Johnson acceded, and the original members were, Sir Joshua Reynolds, Dr. Johnson, Mr. Edmund Burke, Dr. Nugent, Mr. Beauclerk, Mr. Langton, Dr. Goldsmith, Mr. Chamier, and Sir John Hawkins. They met at the Turk's Head, in Gerrard-street, Soho, one evening in every week, at seven, and generally continued their conversation till a pretty late hour. This club has been gradually increased to its present number, thirty-five. After about ten years, instead of supping weekly, it was resolved to dine together once a fortnight during the meeting of Parliament. Their original tavern having been converted into a private house, they moved first to Prince's in Sackville-street, then to Le Telier's in Dover-street, and now meet at Parsloe's, St. James's-street.

⚹ ⚹⚹45. *Johnson's Singularities* [1764].

He had another particularity, of which none of his friends ever ventured to ask an explanation. It appeared to me some superstitious habit, which he had contracted early, and from which he had never called upon his reason to disentangle him. This was his anxious care to go out or in at a door or passage, by a certain number of steps from a certain point, or at least so as that either his right or his left foot, (I am not certain which,) should constantly make the first actual movement when he came close to the door or passage. Thus I conjecture: for I have, upon innumerable occasions, observed him suddenly stop, and then seem to count his steps with a deep earnestness; and when he had neglected or gone wrong in this sort of magical movement, I have seen him go back again, put himself in a proper posture to begin the ceremony, and, having gone through it, break from his abstraction, walk briskly on, and join his companion. A strange instance of something of this nature, even when on horseback, happened when he was in the isle of Sky. Sir Joshua Reynolds has observed him to go a good way about, rather than cross a particular alley in Leicester-fields; but this Sir Joshua imputed to his having had some disagreeable recollection associated with it.

That the most minute singularities which belonged to him, and made very observable parts of his appearance and manner, may not be omitted, it is requisite to mention, that while talking or even musing as he sat in his chair, he commonly held his head to one side towards his right shoulder, and shook it in a tremulous manner, moving his body backwards and forwards, and rubbing his left knee in the same direction, with the palm of his hand. In the intervals of articulating he made various sounds with his mouth, sometimes as if ruminating, or what is called chewing the cud, sometimes giving a half whistle, sometimes making his tongue play backwards from the roof of his mouth, as if clucking like a hen, and sometimes protruding it against his upper gums in front, as if pronouncing quickly under his breath, *too*, *too*, *too*: all this accompanied sometimes with a thoughtful look, but more frequently with a smile. Generally when he had concluded a period, in the course of a dispute, by which time he was a good deal exhausted by violence and vociferation, he used to blow out his breath like a Whale. This I suppose was a relief to his lungs; and seemed in him to be a contemptuous mode of expression, as if he had made the arguments of his opponent fly like chaff before the wind.

46. *Letter to Reynolds* [1765].

'To Joshua Reynolds, Esq., in Leicester-fields, London.

'Dear Sir,—I did not hear of your sickness till I heard likewise of your recovery, and therefore escaped that part of your pain, which every man must feel, to whom you are known as you are known to me.

'Having had no particular account of your disorder, I know not in what state it has left you. If the amusement of my company can exhilarate the languor of a slow recovery, I will not delay a day to come to you; for I know not how I can so effectually promote my own pleasure as by pleasing you, or my own interest as by preserving you, in whom, if I should lose you, I should lose almost the only man whom I call a friend.

'Pray let me hear of you from yourself, or from dear Miss Reynolds [1]. Make my compliments to Mr. Mudge. I am, dear Sir, your most affectionate and most humble servant,

'At the Rev. Mr. Percy's, at Easton   'SAM JOHNSON.'
Maudit, Northamptonshire, (by
Castle Ashby,) Aug. 19, 1764.'

47. *The Thrales* [1765].

This year was distinguished by his being introduced into the family of Mr. Thrale, one of the most eminent brewers in England, and Member of Parliament for the borough of Southwark. Foreigners are not a little amazed when they hear of brewers, distillers, and men in similar departments of trade, held forth

---

[1] Sir Joshua's sister, for whom Johnson had a particular affection, and to whom he wrote many letters which I have seen, and which I am sorry her too nice delicacy will not permit to be published.

as persons of considerable consequence. In this great commercial country it is natural that a situation which produces much wealth should be considered as very respectable; and, no doubt, honest industry is entitled to esteem. But, perhaps, the too rapid advance of men of low extraction tends to lessen the value of that distinction by birth and gentility, which has ever been found beneficial to the grand scheme of subordination. . . . .

Mr. Thrale had married Miss Hesther Lynch Salusbury, of good Welch extraction, a lady of lively talents, improved by education. That Johnson's introduction into Mr. Thrale's family, which contributed so much to the happiness of his life, was owing to her desire for his conversation, is very probable, and a general supposition: but it is not the truth. Mr. Murphy, who was intimate with Mr. Thrale, having spoken very highly of Dr. Johnson, he was requested to make them acquainted. This being mentioned to Johnson, he accepted of an invitation to dinner at Thrale's and was so much pleased with his reception, both by Mr. and Mrs. Thrale, and they so much pleased with him, that his invitations to their house were more and more frequent, till at last he became one of the family, and an apartment was appropriated to him, both in their house in Southwark and in their villa at Streatham. . . . .

Nothing could be more fortunate for Johnson than this connection. He had at Mr. Thrale's all the comforts and even luxuries of life; his melancholy was diverted, and his irregular habits lessened by association with an agreeable and well-ordered family. He was treated with the utmost respect, and even affection. The vivacity of Mrs. Thrale's literary talk roused him to cheerfulness and exertion, even when they were alone. But this was not often the case; for he found here a constant succession of what gave him the highest enjoyment: the society of the learned, the witty, and the eminent in every way, who were assembled in numerous companies, called forth his wonderful powers, and gratified him with admiration, to which no man could be insensible.

48. *Making Verses* [1766].

He talked of making verses, and observed, The great difficulty is to know when you have made good ones. When composing, I have generally had them in my mind, perhaps fifty at a time, walking up and down in my room; and then I have written them down, and often, from laziness, have written only half lines. I have written a hundred lines in a day. I remember I wrote a hundred lines of *The Vanity of Human Wishes* in a day. Doctor, (turning to Goldsmith,) I am not quite idle; I made one line t'other day; but I made no more.' GOLDSMITH. 'Let us hear it; we'll put a bad one to it.' JOHNSON. 'No, Sir, I have forgot it.'

Such specimens of the easy and playful conversation of the great Dr. Samuel Johnson are, I think, to be prized; as exhibiting the little varieties of a mind so enlarged and so powerful when objects of consequence required its exertions, and as giving us a minute knowledge of his character and modes of thinking.

49. *On Translating the Bible into Gaelic* [1766].

He wrote this year a letter, not intended for publication, which has, perhaps, as strong marks of his sentiment and style, as any of his compositions. The original is in my possession. It is addressed to the late Mr. William Drummond, bookseller in Edinburgh, a gentleman of good family, but small estate, who took arms for the house of Stuart in 1745; and during his concealment in London till the act of general pardon came out, obtained the acquaintance of Dr. Johnson, who justly esteemed him as a very worthy man. It seems, some of the members of the society in Scotland for propagating Christian knowledge, had opposed the scheme ot translating the holy scriptures into the Erse or Gaelick language, from political considerations of the dis-advantage of keeping up the distinction between the Highlanders and the other inhabitants of North-Britain. Dr. Johnson being informed of this, I suppose by Mr. Drummond, wrote with a generous indignation as follows :

' To Mr. William Drummond.

'Sir,—I did not expect to hear that it could be, in an assembly convened for the propagation of Christian knowledge, a question whether any nation uninstructed in religion should receive instruction; or whether that instruction should be imparted to them by a translation of the holy books into their

own language.   If obedience to the will of GOD be
necessary to happiness, and knowledge of his will
be necessary to obedience, I know not how he that
with-holds this knowledge, or delays it, can be said to
love his neighbour as himself.   He, that voluntarily
continues ignorance, is guilty of all the crimes which
ignorance produces; as to him that should extinguish
the tapers of a light-house, might justly be imputed
the calamities of shipwrecks.   Christianity is the
highest perfection of humanity; and as no man is
good but as he wishes the good of others, no man
can be good in the highest degree, who wishes not
to others the largest measures of the greatest good.
To omit for a year, or for a day, the most efficacious
method of advancing Christianity, in compliance with
any purposes that terminate on this side of the grave, is
a crime of which I know not that the world has yet
had an example, except in the practice of the planters
of America, a race of mortals whom, I suppose, no
other man wishes to resemble.

'The Papists have, indeed, denied to the laity the
use of the bible; but this prohibition, in few places
now very rigorously enforced, is defended by arguments, which have for their foundation the care of
souls.   To obscure, upon motives merely political, the
light of revelation, is a practice reserved for the
reformed; and, surely, the blackest midnight of popery
is meridian sunshine to such a reformation.   I am not
very willing that any language should be totally extinguished.   The similitude and derivation of languages
afford the most indubitable proof of the traduction

of nations, and the genealogy of mankind. They add often physical certainty to historical evidence; and often supply the only evidence of ancient migrations, and of the revolutions of ages which left no written monuments behind them.

' Every man's opinions, at least his desires, are a little influenced by his favourite studies. My zeal for languages may seem, perhaps, rather over-heated, even to those by whom I desire to be well-esteemed. To those who have nothing in their thoughts but trade or policy, present power, or present money, I should not think it necessary to defend my opinions; but with men of letters I would not unwillingly compound, by wishing the continuance of every language, however narrow in its extent, or however incommodious for common purposes, till it is reposited in some version of a known book, that it may be always hereafter examined and compared with other languages, and then permitting its disuse. For this purpose, the translation of the bible is most to be desired. It is not certain that the same method will not preserve the Highland language, for the purposes of learning, and abolish it from daily use. When the Highlanders read the Bible, they will naturally wish to have its obscurities cleared, and to know the history, collateral or appendant. Knowledge always desires increase: it is like fire, which must first be kindled by some external agent, but which will afterwards propagate itself. When they once desire to learn, they will naturally have recourse to the nearest language by which that desire can be gratified; and one will tell another that if he would attain knowledge, he must learn English.

'This speculation may, perhaps, be thought more subtle than the grossness of real life will easily admit. Let it, however, be remembered, that the efficacy of ignorance has been long tried, and has not produced the consequence expected. Let knowledge, therefore, take its turn ; and let the patrons of privation stand awhile aside, and admit the operation of positive principles.

'You will be pleased, Sir, to assure the worthy man who is employed in the new translation, that he has my wishes for his success ; and if here or at Oxford I can be of any use, that I shall think it more than honour to promote his undertaking.

'I am sorry that I delayed so long to write. I am, Sir, your most humble servant,

'Johnson's-court, Fleet-street, 'SAM. JOHNSON.'
      Aug. 13, 1766.'

The opponents of this pious scheme being made ashamed of their conduct, the benevolent undertaking was allowed to go on.

50. *Interview with George III* [1767].

In February, 1767, there happened one of the most remarkable incidents of Johnson's life, which gratified his monarchical enthusiasm, and which he loved to relate with all its circumstances, when requested by his friends. This was his being honoured by a private conversation with his Majesty, in the library at the Queen's house. He had frequently visited those splendid rooms and noble collection of books, which he used to say was more numerous and curious than he supposed any person could have made in the time which the King had employed. Mr. Barnard, the librarian, took care that he should have every accommodation that could contribute to his ease and convenience, while indulging his literary taste in that place ; so that he had here a very agreeable resource at leisure hours.

His Majesty having been informed of his occasional visits, was pleased to signify a desire that he should be told when Dr. Johnson came next to the library. Accordingly, the next time that Johnson did come, as soon as he was fairly engaged with a book, on which, while he sat by the fire, he seemed quite intent, Mr. Barnard stole round to the apartment where the King was, and, in obedience to his Majesty's commands, mentioned that Dr. Johnson was then in the library. His Majesty said he was at leisure, and would go to him ; upon which Mr. Barnard took one of the candles that stood on the King's table, and lighted his Majesty through a suite of rooms, till they came to a private door into the library, of which his Majesty had the key. Being entered, Mr. Barnard stepped forward hastily to Dr. Johnson, who was still in a profound study, and whispered him, ' Sir, here is the King.' Johnson started up, and stood still. His Majesty approached him, and at once was courteously easy.

His Majesty began by observing, that he understood he came sometimes to the library ; and then mentioning his having heard that the Doctor had been lately at Oxford, asked him if he was not fond of going thither. To which Johnson answered, that he was indeed fond of going to Oxford sometimes, but was likewise glad to come back again. The King then asked him what they were doing at Oxford. Johnson answered, he could not much commend their diligence, but that in some respects they were mended, for they had put their press under better regulations, and were at that time printing Polybius. He was then asked whether there were better libraries at Oxford or Cambridge. He answered, he believed the Bodleian was larger than any they had at Cambridge; at the same time adding, ' I hope, whether we have more books or not than they have at Cambridge, we shall make as good use of them as they do.' Being asked whether All-Souls or Christ-Church library was the largest, he answered, ' All-Souls library is the largest we have, except the Bodleian.' ' Aye, (said the King,) that is the publick library.'

His Majesty enquired if he was then writing any thing. He answered, he was not, for he had pretty well told the world what he knew, and must now read to acquire more knowledge. The King, as it should seem with a view to urge him to rely on his own stores as an original writer, and to continue his labours, then said ' I do not think you borrow much from any body.' Johnson said, he thought he had already done his part as a writer. ' I should have thought so too, (said the King,) if you had not written so well.'—Johnson observed to me, upon this, that

'No man could have paid a handsomer compliment;
and it was fit for a King to pay. It was decisive.'
When asked by another friend, at Sir Joshua
Reynolds's, whether he made any reply to this high
compliment, he answered, ' No, Sir. When the King
had said it, it was to be so. It was not for me to
bandy civilities with my Sovereign.' Perhaps no man
who had spent his whole life in courts could have
shewn a more nice and dignified sense of true politeness, than Johnson did in this instance. . . . .

At Sir Joshua Reynolds's, where a circle of Johnson's
friends was collected round him to hear his account
of this memorable conversation, Dr. Joseph Warton,
in his frank and lively manner, was very active in
pressing him to mention the particulars. 'Come
now, Sir, this is an interesting matter; do favour us
with it.' Johnson, with great good humour, com-
plied. . . . .

During all the time in which Dr. Johnson was
employed in relating to the circle at Sir Joshua
Reynolds's the particulars of what passed between the
King and him, Dr. Goldsmith remained unmoved upon
a sopha at some distance, affecting not to join in the
least in the eager curiosity of the company. He
assigned as a reason for his gloom and seeming inatten-
tion, that he apprehended Johnson had relinquished
his purpose of furnishing him with a Prologue to his
play, with the hopes of which he had been flattered;
but it was strongly suspected that he was fretting with
chagrin and envy at the singular honour Dr. Johnson
had lately enjoyed. At length, the frankness, and

simplicity of his natural character prevailed. He sprung from the sopha, advanced to Johnson, and in a kind of flutter, from imagining himself in the situation which he had just been hearing described, exclaimed, 'Well, you acquitted yourself in this conversation better than I should have done; for I should have bowed and stammered through the whole of it.'

✳ 51. *Conglobulation of Swallows* [1767].

He seemed pleased to talk of natural philosophy. 'That woodcocks, (said he,) fly over to the northern countries, is proved, because they have been observed at sea. Swallows certainly sleep all the winter. A number of them conglobulate together, by flying round and round, and then all in a heap throw themselves under water, and lye in the bed of a river.'

52. *Corsica* [1768].

He remained at Oxford a considerable time; I was obliged to go to London, where I received his letter, which had been returned from Scotland.

'To JAMES BOSWELL, ESQ.

'MY DEAR BOSWELL,—I have omitted a long time to write to you, without knowing very well why. I could now tell why I should not write; for who would write to men who publish the letters of their friends, without their leave? Yet I write to you in spite of my caution, to tell you that I shall be glad to see you, and that I wish you would empty your head of Corsica, which I think has filled it rather too long. But, at all

events, I shall be glad, very glad to see you.   I am,
Sir, yours affectionately,
  'Oxford, March 23, 1768'.   'SAM. JOHNSON.'

I answered thus :

  'TO MR. SAMUEL JOHNSON.

'MY DEAR SIR,   'London, 26th April, 1768.
  'I have received your last letter, which, though
very short, and by no means complimentary, yet gave
me real pleasure, because it contains these words, "I
shall be glad, very glad to see you." Surely you have
no reason to complain of my publishing a single para-
graph of one of your letters; the temptation to it was
so strong. An irrevocable grant of your friendship, and
your dignifying my desire of visiting Corsica with the
epithet of "a wise and noble curiosity," are to me
more valuable than many of the grants of kings.
  'But how can you bid me "empty my head of
Corsica?" My noble-minded friend, do you not feel
for an oppressed nation bravely struggling to be free?
Consider fairly what is the case. The Corsicans never
received any kindness from the Genoese. They never
agreed to be subject to them. They owe them
nothing; and when reduced to an abject state of
slavery, by force, shall they not rise in the great cause
of liberty, and break the galling yoke? And shall not
every liberal soul be warm for them? Empty my head
of Corsica! Empty it of honour, empty it of humanity,
empty it of friendship, empty it of piety. No! while I
live, Corsica and the cause of the brave islanders shall

ever employ much of my attention, shall ever interest me in the sincerest manner. . . . I am, &c.

'JAMES BOSWELL.'

53. *Nothing of the Bear but his Skin* [1768].

To obviate all the reflections which have gone round the world to Johnson's prejudice, by applying to him the epithet of a *bear*, let me impress upon my readers a just and happy saying of my friend Goldsmith, who knew him well : 'Johnson, to be sure, has a roughness in his manner ; but no man alive has a more tender heart. *He has nothing of the bear but his skin.*'

54. *Letter to Boswell* [1769].

From Brighthelmstone Dr. Johnson wrote me the following letter, which they who may think that I ought to have suppressed, must have less ardent feelings than I have always avowed.

'TO JAMES BOSWELL, ESQ.

'DEAR SIR,—Why do you charge me with unkindness ? I have omitted nothing that could do you good, or give you pleasure, unless it be that I have forborne to tell you my opinion of your *Account of Corsica.* I believe my opinion, if you think well of my judgement, might have given you pleasure ; but when it is considered how much vanity is excited by praise, I am not sure that it would have done you good. Your History is like other histories, but your Journal is in a very high degree curious and delightful. There is between the History and the Journal that difference which there will always be found between notions borrowed from without, and notions generated within. Your History was copied from books; your Journal rose out of your own experience and observation. You express images which operated strongly upon yourself, and you have impressed them with great force upon your readers.   I know not whether I could name any narrative by which curiosity is better excited, or better gratified.

'I am glad that you are going to be married; and as I wish you well in things of less importance, wish you well with proportionate ardour in this crisis of your life.   What I can contribute to your happiness, I should be very unwilling to with-hold; for I have always loved and valued you, and shall love you and value you still more, as you become more regular and useful: effects which a happy marriage will hardly fail to produce.

'I do not find that I am likely to come back very soon from this place.   I shall, perhaps, stay a fortnight longer; and a fortnight is a long time to a lover absent from his mistress.   Would a fortnight ever have an end? I am, dear Sir, your most affectionate humble servant,

'Brighthelmstone, Sept. 9, 1769.'   'SAM. JOHNSON.'

55. *Garrick and Goldsmith* [1769].

He honoured me with his company at dinner on the 16th of October, at my lodgings in Old Bond-street, with Sir Joshua Reynolds, Mr. Garrick, Dr. Goldsmith,

Mr. Murphy, Mr. Bickerstaff, and Mr. Thomas Davies. Garrick played round him with a fond vivacity, taking hold of the breasts of his coat, and, looking up in his face with a lively archness, complimented him on the good health which he seemed then to enjoy; while the sage, shaking his head, beheld him with a gentle complacency. One of the company not being come at the appointed hour, I proposed, as usual upon such occasions to order dinner to be served; adding, 'Ought six people to be kept waiting for one?' 'Why, yes, (answered Johnson, with a delicate humanity,) if the one will suffer more by your sitting down, than the six will do by waiting.' Goldsmith, to divert the tedious minutes, strutted about, bragging of his dress, and I believe was seriously vain of it, for his mind was wonderfully prone to such impressions. 'Come, come, (said Garrick,) talk no more of that. You are, perhaps, the worst—eh, eh!'—Goldsmith was eagerly attempting to interrupt him, when Garrick went on, laughing ironically, 'Nay, you will always *look* like a gentleman; but I am talking of being well or *ill drest.*' 'Well, let me tell you, (said Goldsmith,) when my tailor brought home my bloom-coloured coat, he said, "Sir, I have a favour to beg of you. When any body asks you who made your clothes, be pleased to mention John Filby, at the Harrow, in Water-lane."' JOHNSON. 'Why, Sir, that was because he knew the strange colour would attract crouds to gaze at it, and thus they might hear of him, and see how well he could make a coat even of so absurd a colour.'

56. *Real Criticism* [1769].

Mrs. Montagu, a lady distinguished for having written an Essay on Shakespeare, being mentioned; REYNOLDS. 'I think that essay does her honour.' JOHNSON. 'Yes, Sir; it does *her* honour, but it would do nobody else honour. I have, indeed, not read it all. But when I take up the end of a web, and find it packthread, I do not expect, by looking further, to find embroidery. Sir, I will venture to say, there is not one sentence of true criticism in her book.' GARRICK. 'But, Sir, surely it shews how much Voltaire has mistaken Shakespeare, which nobody else has done.' JOHNSON. 'Sir, nobody else has thought it worth while. And what merit is there in that? You may as well praise a schoolmaster for whipping a boy who has construed ill. No, Sir, there is no real criticism in it: none shewing the beauty of thought, as formed on the workings of the human heart.' . . . .

JOHNSON. 'We have an example of true criticism in Burke's *Essay on the Sublime and Beautiful*; and, if I recollect, there is also Du Bos; and Bouhours, who shews all beauty to depend on truth. There is no great merit in telling how many plays have ghosts in them, and how this Ghost is better than that. You must shew how terrour is impressed on the human heart.—In the description of night in *Macbeth*, the beetle and the bat detract from the general idea of darkness,—inspissated gloom.'

57. *Death* [1769].

To my question, whether we might not fortify our minds for the approach of death, he answered, in a passion, 'No, Sir, let it alone. It matters not how a man dies, but how he lives. The act of dying is not of importance, it lasts so short a time.' He added, (with an earnest look,) 'A man knows it must be so, and submits. It will do him no good to whine.'

I attempted to continue the conversation. He was so provoked, that he said, 'Give us no more of this;' and was thrown into such a state of agitation, that he expressed himself in a way that alarmed and distressed me; shewed an impatience that I should leave him, and when I was going away, called to me sternly, 'Don't let us meet to-morrow.'

58. *Apple Dumplins* [1770. *Communicated by Dr. Maxwell*].

'He advised me, if possible, to have a good orchard. He knew, he said, a clergyman of small income, who brought up a family very reputably, which he chiefly fed with apple dumplins.'

59. *Mimickry* [1772].

I gave him an account of the excellent mimickry of a friend of mine in Scotland; observing, at the same time, that some people thought it a very mean thing. JOHNSON. 'Why, Sir, it is making a very mean use of a man's powers. But to be a good mimick, requires great powers; great acuteness of observation, great retention of what is observed, and great pliancy of organs, to represent what is observed. I remember a lady of quality in this town, Lady————————, who was a wonderful mimick, and used to make me laugh immoderately. I have heard she is now gone mad.' BOSWELL. 'It is amazing how a mimick can not only give you the gestures and voice of a person whom he represents; but even what a person would say on any particular subject.' JOHNSON. 'Why, Sir, you are to consider that the manner and some particular phrases of a person do much to impress you with an idea of him, and you are not sure that he would say what the mimick says in his character.' BOSWELL. 'I don't think Foote a good mimick, Sir.' JOHNSON. 'No, Sir; his imitations are not like. He gives you something different from himself, but not the character which he means to assume. He goes out of himself, without going into other people. He cannot take off any person unless he is strongly marked, such as George Faulkner. He is like a painter, who can draw the portrait of a man who has a wen upon his face, and who, therefore, is easily known. If a man hops upon one leg, Foote can hop upon one leg. But he has not that nice discrimination which your friend seems to possess. Foote is, however, very entertaining, with a kind of conversation between wit and buffoonery.'

60. *The Dictionary* [1772].

On Monday, March 23, I found him busy, preparing a fourth edition of his folio Dictionary. Mr. Peyton, one of his original amanuenses, was writing for him. I put him in mind of a meaning of the word *side*, which he had omitted, viz. relationship; as father's side, mother's side. He inserted it. I asked him if *humiliating* was a good word. He said, he had seen it frequently used, but he did not know it to be legitimate English. He would not admit *civilization*, but only *civility*. With great deference to him, I thought *civilization*, from *to civilize* better in the sense opposed to *barbarity*, than *civility*; as it is better to have a distinct word for each sense, than one word with two senses, which *civility* is, in his way of using it.

61. *Scotch Accents* [1772].

SIR A[LEXANDER MACDONALD]. ' I have been correcting several Scotch accents in my friend Boswell. I doubt, Sir, if any Scotchman ever attains to a perfect English pronunciation.' JOHNSON. 'Why, Sir, few of them do, because they do not persevere after acquiring a certain degree of it. But, Sir, there can be no doubt that they may attain to a perfect English pronunciation, if they will. We find how near they come to it; and certainly, a man who conquers nineteen parts of the Scottish accent, may conquer the twentieth. But, Sir, when a man has got the better of nine tenths he grows weary, he relaxes his diligence, he finds he has corrected his accent so far as not to be disagreeable, and he no longer desires his friends to tell him when he is wrong; nor does he choose to be told. Sir, when people watch me narrowly, and I do not watch myself, they will find me out to be of a particular county. In the same manner, Dunning may be found out to be a Devonshire man. So most Scotchmen may be found out. But, Sir, little aberrations are of no disadvantage. I never catched Mallet in a Scotch accent; and yet Mallet, I suppose, was past five-and-twenty before he came to London.'

Upon another occasion I talked to him on this subject, having myself taken some pains to improve my pronunciation, by the aid of the late Mr. Love, of Drurylane theatre, when he was a player at Edinburgh, and also of old Mr. Sheridan. Johnson said to me, 'Sir, your pronunciation is not offensive.'

62. *A Vile Whig* [1772].

Sir Adam [Fergusson] suggested, that luxury corrupts a people, and destroys the spirit of liberty. JOHNSON. 'Sir, that is all visionary. I would not give half a guinea to live under one form of government rather than another. It is of no moment to the happiness of an individual. Sir, the danger of the abuse of power is nothing to a private man. What Frenchman is prevented from passing his life as he pleases?' SIR ADAM. 'But, Sir, in the British constitution it is surely of importance to keep up a spirit in the people, so as to preserve a balance against the crown.' JOHNSON. 'Sir, I perceive you are a vile Whig.—Why all this childish jealousy of the power of the crown? The crown has not power enough. When I say that all governments are alike, I consider that in no government power can be abused long. Mankind will not bear it. If a sovereign oppresses his people to a great degree, they will rise and cut off his head. There is a remedy in human nature against tyranny, that will keep us safe under every form of government. Had not the people of France thought themselves honoured as sharing in the brilliant actions of Lewis XIV. they would not have endured him; and we may say the same of the King of Prussia's people.' Sir Adam introduced the ancient Greeks and Romans. JOHNSON. 'Sir, the mass of both of them were barbarians. The mass of every people must be barbarous where there is no printing, and consequently knowledge is not generally diffused. Knowledge is diffused among our people by the news-papers.' Sir Adam mentioned the orators, poets, and artists of Greece. JOHNSON. 'Sir, I am talking of the mass of the people. We see even what the boasted Athenians were. The little effect which Demosthenes's orations had upon them, shews that they were barbarians.'

63. *Goldsmith* [1772].

Of our friend Goldsmith he said, 'Sir, he is so much afraid of being unnoticed, that he often talks merely lest you should forget that he is in the company.' BOSWELL. 'Yes, he stands forward.' JOHNSON. 'True, Sir; but if a man is to stand forward, he should wish to do it not in an aukward posture, not in rags, not so as that he shall only be exposed to ridicule.' BOSWELL. 'For my part, I like very well to hear honest Goldsmith talk away carelessly.' JOHNSON. 'Why yes, Sir; but he should not like to hear himself.'

64. *Scotchmen* [1772].

He would not allow Scotland to derive any credit from Lord Mansfield ; for he was educated in England. ' Much (said he,) may be made of a Scotchman, if he be *caught* young.'

65. *Goldsmith* [1772].

' The misfortune of Goldsmith in conversation is this : he goes on without knowing how he is to get off. His genius is great, but his knowledge is small. As they say of a generous man, it is a pity he is not rich, we may say of Goldsmith, it is a pity he is not knowing. He would not keep his knowledge to himself.'

66. *Letter to Boswell* [1773].

To James Boswell, Esq.

'Dear Sir,—I have read your kind letter much more than the elegant *Pindar* which it accompanied. I am always glad to find myself not forgotten ; and to be forgotten by you would give me great uneasiness. My northern friends have never been unkind to me : I have from you, dear Sir, testimonies of affection, which I have not often been able to excite ; and Dr. Beattie rates the testimony which I was desirous of paying to his merit, much higher than I should have thought it reasonable to expect. . . . . .

' A new edition of my great *Dictionary* is printed, from a copy which I was persuaded to revise ; but having made no preparation, I was able to do very little. Some superfluities I have expunged, and some faults I have corrected, and here and there have scattered a remark; but the main fabrick of the work remains as it was. I had looked very little into it since I wrote it, and, I think, I found it full as often better, as worse, than I expected.

'Baretti and Davies have had a furious quarrel; a quarrel, I think, irreconcileable. Dr. Goldsmith has a new comedy, which is expected in the spring. No name is yet given it. The chief diversion arises from a stratagem by which a lover is made to mistake his future father-in-law's house for an inn. This, you see, borders upon farce. The dialogue is quick and gay, and the incidents are so prepared as not to seem improbable.'

67. *Gesticulation* [1773].

At Mr. Thrale's, in the evening, he repeated his usual paradoxical declamation against action in publick speaking. 'Action can have no effect upon reasonable minds. It may augment noise, but it never can enforce argument. If you speak to a dog, you use action; you hold up your hand thus, because he is a brute; and in proportion as men are removed from brutes, action will have the less influence upon them.' MRS. THRALE. 'What then, Sir, becomes of Demosthenes's saying? "Action, action, action!"' JOHNSON. 'Demosthenes, Madam, spoke to an assembly of brutes; to a barbarous people.'

68. *Lord Chesterfield* [1773].

Lord Chesterfield being mentioned, Johnson remarked, that almost all of that celebrated nobleman's witty sayings were puns. He, however, allowed the merit of good wit to his Lordship's saying of Lord Tyrawley and himself, when both very old and infirm : ' Tyrawley and I have been dead these two years ; but we don't choose to have it known.'

69. *Goldsmith* [1773].

I told him that Goldsmith had said to me a few days before, ' As I take my shoes from the shoemaker, and my coat from the taylor, so I take my religion from the priest.'   I regretted this loose way of talking. JOHNSON. ' Sir, he knows nothing; he has made up his mind about nothing.'

70. *Reading Books Through* [1773].

Mr. Elphinston talked of a new book that was much admired, and asked Dr. Johnson if he had read it. JOHNSON. 'I have looked into it.' 'What, (said Elphinston,) have you not read it through ?' Johnson, offended at being thus pressed, and so obliged to own his cursory mode of reading, answered tartly, ' No, Sir ; do *you* read books *through* ? '

71. *Goldsmith* [1773].

He said, ' Goldsmith should not be for ever attempting to shine in conversation: he has not temper for it, he is so much mortified when he fails.   Sir, a game of jokes is composed partly of skill, partly of chance, a man may be beat at times by one who has not the tenth part of his wit.   Now Goldsmith's putting himself against another, is like a man laying a hundred to one who cannot spare the hundred. It is not worth a man's while. A man should not lay a hundred to one, unless he can easily spare it, though he has a hundred chances for him: he can get but a guinea, and he may lose a hundred. Goldsmith is in this state. When he contends, if he gets the better, it is a very little addition to a man of his literary reputation: if he does not get the better, he is miserably vexed.' . . . .

Goldsmith, however, was often very fortunate in his witty contests, even when he entered the lists with Johnson himself. Sir Joshua Reynolds was in company with them one day, when Goldsmith said, that he thought he could write a good fable, mentioned the simplicity which that kind of composition requires, and observed, that in most fables the animals introduced seldom talk in character. 'For instance, (said he,) the fable of the little fishes, who saw birds fly over their heads, and envying them, petitioned Jupiter to be changed into birds. The skill (continued he,) consists in making them talk like little fishes.' While he indulged himself in this fanciful reverie, he observed Johnson shaking his sides, and laughing. Upon which he smartly proceeded, 'Why, Dr. Johnson, this is not so easy as you seem to think; for if you were to make little fishes talk, they would talk like WHALES.'

72. *Historians* [1773].

Goldsmith being mentioned; JOHNSON. 'It is amazing how little Goldsmith knows. He seldom comes where he is not more ignorant than any one else.'

SIR JOSHUA REYNOLDS. 'Yet there is no man whose company is more liked.' JOHNSON. 'To be sure, Sir. When people find a man of the most distinguished abilities as a writer, their inferiour while he is with them, it must be highly gratifying to them. What Goldsmith comically says of himself is very true,—he always gets the better when he argues alone; meaning, that he is master of a subject in his study, and can write well upon it; but when he comes into company, grows confused, and unable to talk. Take him as a poet, his *Traveller* is a very fine performance; ay, and so is his *Deserted Village*, were it not sometimes too much the echo of his *Traveller*. Whether, indeed, we take him as a poet,—as a comick writer,—or as an historian, he stands in the first class.' BOSWELL. 'An historian! My dear Sir, you surely will not rank his compilation of the Roman History with the works of other historians of his age?' JOHNSON. 'Why, who are before him?' BOSWELL. 'Hume,—Robertson,—Lord Lyttleton.' JOHNSON. (His antipathy to the Scotch beginning to rise,) 'I have not read Hume; but, doubtless, Goldsmith's *History* is better than the *verbiage* of Robertson, or the foppery of Dalrymple.' BOSWELL. 'Will you not admit the superiority of Robertson, in whose *History* we find such penetration—such painting?' JOHNSON. 'Sir, you must consider how that penetration and that painting are employed. It is not history, it is imagination. He who describes what he never saw, draws from fancy. Robertson paints minds as Sir Joshua paints faces in a history-piece: he imagines an heroick countenance.

You must look upon Robertson's work as romance, and try it by that standard. History it is not. Besides, Sir, it is the great excellence of a writer to put into his book as much as his book will hold. Goldsmith has done this in his *History*. Now Robertson might have put twice as much into his book. Robertson is like a man who has packed gold in wool: the wool takes up more room than the gold. No, Sir; I always thought Robertson would be crushed by his own weight,— would be buried under his own ornaments. Goldsmith tells you shortly all you want to know: Robertson detains you a great deal too long. No man will read Robertson's cumbrous detail a second time; but Goldsmith's plain narrative will please again and again. I would say to Robertson what an old tutor of a college said to one of his pupils: "Read over your compositions, and where ever you meet with a passage which you think is particularly fine, strike it out." Goldsmith's abridgement is better than that of Lucius Florus or Eutropius; and I will venture to say, that if you compare him with Vertot, in the same places of the Roman History, you will find that he excels Vertot. Sir, he has the art of compiling, and of saying every thing he has to say in a pleasing manner. He is now writing a Natural History and will make it as entertaining as a Persian Tale.'

73. *Boswell's Election to the Club* [1773].

The gentlemen went away to their club, and I was left at Beauclerk's till the fate of my election should be announced to me. I sat in a state of anxiety which even the charming conversation of Lady Di Beauclerk could not entirely dissipate.   In a short time I received the agreeable intelligence that I was chosen. I hastened to the place of meeting, and was introduced to such a society as can seldom be found.   Mr. Edmund Burke, whom I then saw for the first time, and whose splendid talents had long made me ardently wish for his acquaintance; Dr. Nugent, Mr. Garrick, Dr. Goldsmith, Mr. (afterwards Sir William) Jones, and the company with whom I had dined.   Upon my entrance, Johnson placed himself behind a chair, on which he leaned as on a desk or pulpit, and with humorous formality gave me a *Charge*, pointing out the conduct expected from me as a good member of this club.

74. *The Migration of Birds* [1773].

Talking of birds, I mentioned Mr. Daines Barrington's ingenious Essay against the received notion of their migration. JOHNSON. ' I think we have as good evidence for the migration of woodcocks as can be desired.   We find they disappear at a certain time of the year, and appear again at a certain time of the year ; and some of them, when weary in their flight, have been known to alight on the rigging of ships far out at sea.'   One of the company observed, that there had been instances of some of them found in summer in Essex. JOHNSON. ' Sir, that strengthens our argument. *Exceptio probat regulam.* Some being found shews, that, if all remained, many would be found.   A few sick or lame ones may be found.' GOLDSMITH.   ' There is a partial migration of the swallows ; the stronger ones migrate, the others do not.'

75. *The Government of Ireland* [1773].

BOSWELL. ' Pray, Mr. Dilly, how does Dr. Leland's *History of Ireland* sell ? ' JOHNSON. (bursting forth with a generous indignation,) ' The Irish are in a most unnatural state; for we see there the minority prevailing over the majority. There is no instance, even in the ten persecutions, of such severity as that which the protestants of Ireland have exercised against the Catholicks. Did we tell them we have conquered them, it would be above board : to punish them by confiscation and other penalties, as rebels, was monstrous injustice. King William was not their lawful sovereign : he had not been acknowledged by the Parliament of Ireland, when they appeared in arms against him.'

76. *Goldy* [1773].

In our way to the club to-night, when I regretted that Goldsmith would, upon every occasion, endeavour to shine, by which he often exposed himself, Mr. Langton observed, that he was not like Addison, who was content with the fame of his writings, and did not aim also at excellency in conversation, for which he found himself unfit; and that he said to a lady who complained of his having talked little in company, ' Madam, I have but ninepence in ready money, but I can draw for a thousand pounds.' I observed, that Goldsmith had a great deal of gold in his cabinet, but, not content with that, was always taking out his purse.

JOHNSON. 'Yes, Sir, and that so often an empty purse!'. . . . .

It may also be observed, that Goldsmith was sometimes content to be treated with an easy familiarity, but, upon occasions, would be consequential and important. An instance of this occurred in a small particular. Johnson had a way of contracting the names of his friends; as Beauclerk, Beau; Boswell, Bozzy; Langton, Lanky; Murphy, Mur; Sheridan, Sherry. I remember one day, when Tom Davies was telling that Dr. Johnson said, 'We are all in labour for a name to *Goldy's* play,' Goldsmith seemed displeased that such a liberty should be taken with his name, and said, 'I have often desired him not to call me *Goldy.*' Tom was remarkably attentive to the most minute circumstance about Johnson. I recollect his telling me once, on my arrival in London, 'Sir, our great friend has made an improvement on his appellation of old Mr. Sheridan. He calls him now *Sherry derry.*'

77. *Copyright* [1773].

On Sunday, May 8, I dined with Johnson at Mr. Langton's with Dr. Beattie and some other company. He descanted on the subject of Literary Property. 'There seems (said he,) to be in authours a stronger right of property than that by occupancy; a metaphysical right, a right, as it were, of creation, which should from its nature be perpetual; but the consent of nations is against it, and indeed reason and the interests of learning are against it; for were it to be perpetual, no book, however useful, could be universally diffused amongst mankind, should the proprietor take it into his head to restrain its circulation. No book could have the advantage of being edited with notes, however necessary to its elucidation, should the proprietor perversely oppose it. For the general good of the world, therefore, whatever valuable work has once been created by an authour, and issued out by him, should be understood as no longer in his power, but as belonging to the publick; at the same time the authour is entitled to an adequate reward. This he should have by an exclusive right to his work for a considerable number of years.'

78. *Journey to the Western Islands* [1773].

His stay in Scotland was from the 18th of August, on which day he arrived, till the 22d of November, when he set out on his return to London; and I believe ninety-four days were never passed by any man in a more vigorous exertion.

He came by the way of Berwick upon Tweed to Edinburgh, where he remained a few days, and then went by St. Andrew's, Aberdeen, Inverness, and Fort Augustus, to the Hebrides, to visit which was the principal object he had in view. He visited the isles of Sky, Rasay, Col, Mull, Inchkenneth, and Icolmkill. He travelled through Argyleshire by Inverary, and from thence by Lochlomond and Dunbarton to Glasgow, then by Loudon to Auchinleck in Ayrshire, the seat of my family, and then by Hamilton, back to Edinburgh, where he again spent some time. He thus saw the four Universities of Scotland, its three principal cities, and

as much of the Highland and insular life as was sufficient for his philosophical contemplation. I had the
pleasure of accompanying him during the whole of
this journey. He was respectfully entertained by the
great, the learned, and the elegant, wherever he went;
nor was he less delighted with the hospitality which he
experienced in humbler life.

His various adventures, and the force and vivacity of
his mind, as exercised during this peregrination, upon
innumerable topicks, have been faithfully, and to the
best of my abilities, displayed in my *Journal of a Tour
to the Hebrides*, to which, as the publick has been
pleased to honour it by a very extensive circulation,
I beg leave to refer, as to a separate and remarkable
portion of his life [1], which may be there seen in detail,
and which exhibits as striking a view of his powers in
conversation, as his works do of his excellence in
writing.

79. *Mrs. Boswell* [1773].

'To JAMES BOSWELL, ESQ.

'DEAR SIR,—I came home last night, without any
incommodity, danger, or weariness, and am ready
to begin a new journey. I shall go to Oxford on

---

[1] The authour was not a small gainer by this extraordinary
Journey; for Dr. Johnson thus writes to Mrs. Thrale, Nov. 3,
1773 :—'Boswell will praise my resolution and perseverance,
and I shall in return celebrate his good humour and perpetual
cheerfulness. He has better faculties than I had imagined;
more justness of discernment, and more fecundity of images. It
is very convenient to travel with him; for there is no house
where he is not received with kindness and respect.' Let. 90, to
Mrs. Thrale. [M.]

Monday. I know Mrs. Boswell wished me well to go[1]; her wishes have not been disappointed. . . . .

'I am, Sir, yours affectionately,

'Nov. 27, 1773.'   'SAM. JOHNSON.'

'TO JAMES BOSWELL, ESQ.

'DEAR SIR, ... Make my compliments to Mrs. Boswell, and tell her that I do not love her the less for wishing me away. I gave her trouble enough, and shall be glad, in recompense, to give her any pleasure.

'I would send some porter into the Hebrides, if I knew which way it could be got to my kind friends there. Enquire, and let me know . . . .

'Jan. 29, 1774.'   'SAM. JOHNSON.'

80. *Fancy and Devotion* [1773. *Letter to Boswell*].

'To what degree fancy is to be admitted into religious offices, it would require much deliberation to determine. I am far from intending totally to exclude it. Fancy is a faculty bestowed by our Creator, and it is reasonable that all his gifts should be used to

---

[1] In this he showed a very acute penetration. My wife paid him the most assiduous and respectful attention, while he was our guest; so that I wonder how he discovered her wishing for his departure. The truth is, that his irregular hours and uncouth habits, such as turning the candles with their heads downwards, when they did not burn bright enough, and letting the wax drop upon the carpet, could not but be disagreeable to a lady. Besides, she had not that high admiration of him which was felt by most of those who knew him; and what was very natural to a female mind, she thought he had too much influence over her husband. She once in a little warmth, made, with more point than justice, this remark upon that subject: 'I have seen many a bear led by a man; but I never before saw a man led by a bear.'

his glory, that all our faculties should co-operate in his worship; but they are to co-operate according to the will of him that gave them, according to the order which his wisdom has established. As ceremonies prudential or convenient are less obligatory than positive ordinances, as bodily worship is only the token to others or ourselves of mental adoration, so Fancy is always to act in subordination to Reason. We may take Fancy for a companion, but must follow Reason as our guide. We may allow Fancy to suggest certain ideas in certain places; but Reason must always be heard, when she tells us, that those ideas and those places have no natural or necessary relation. When we enter a church we habitually recall to mind the duty of adoration, but we must not omit adoration for want of a temple; because we know, and ought to remember, that the Universal Lord is every where present; and that, therefore, to come to Jona, or to Jerusalem, though it may be useful, cannot be necessary.

'Thus I have answered your letter, and have not answered it negligently. I love you too well to be careless when you are serious.'

81. *Goldsmith's Death* [1774. *Letters to . Boswell and Langton*].

'Of poor dear Dr. Goldsmith there is little to be told, more than the papers have made publick. He died of a fever, made, I am afraid, more violent by uneasiness of mind. His debts began to be heavy, and all his resources were exhausted. Sir Joshua is of opinion that he owed not less than two thousand pounds.   Was ever poet so trusted before?' . . . .

'DEAR SIR,—You have reason to reproach me that I have left your last letter so long unanswered, but I had nothing particular to say.   Chambers, you find, is gone far, and poor Goldsmith is gone much further. He died of a fever, exasperated, as I believe, by the fear of distress.   He had raised money and squandered it, by every artifice of acquisition, and folly of expence. But let not his frailties be remembered; he was a very great man.'

82. *Ossian* [1775].

'MR. BOSWELL TO DR. JOHNSON.

'Edinburgh, Feb. 2, 1775.

'. . . . As to Macpherson, I am anxious to have from yourself a full and pointed account of what has passed between you and him.   It is confidently told here, that before your book came out he sent to you, to let you know that he understood you meant to deny the authenticity of Ossian's poems; that the originals were in his possession; that you might have inspection of them, and might take the evidence of people skilled in the Erse language; and that he hoped, after this fair offer, you would not be so uncandid as to assert that he had refused reasonable proof.   That you paid no regard to his message, but published your strong attack upon him; and then he wrote a letter to you, in such terms as he thought suited to one who had not acted as a man of veracity.   You may believe it gives me pain to

hear your conduct represented as unfavourable, while
I can only deny what is said, on the ground that
your character refutes it, without having any information to oppose.   Let me, I beg it of you, be furnished
with a sufficient answer to any calumny upon this
occasion.' . . . .

'TO JAMES BOSWELL, ESQ.

' MY DEAR BOSWELL,—I am surprized that, knowing
as you do the disposition of your countrymen to tell
lies in favour of each other [1], you can be at all affected
by any reports that circulate among them.   Macpherson
never in his life offered me a sight of any original or
of any evidence of any kind; but thought only of
intimidating me by noise and threats, till my last
answer,—that I would not be deterred from detecting
what I thought a cheat, by the menaces of a ruffian
—put an end to our correspondence.

' The state of the question is this.   He, and Dr. Blair,
whom I consider as deceived, say, that he copied the
poem from old manuscripts.   His copies, if he had
them, and I believe him to have none, are nothing.
Where are the manuscripts?   They can be shown if
they exist, but they were never shown.   *De non
existentibus et non apparentibus*, says our law, *eadem
est ratio.*   No man has a claim to credit upon his own
word, when better evidence, if he had it, may be easily
produced.   But, so far as we can find, the Erse language was never written till very lately for the purposes

---

[1] My friend has, in this letter, relied upon my testimony, with
a confidence, of which the ground has escaped my recollection.

of religion. A nation that cannot write, or a language that was never written, has no manuscripts.

'But whatever he has he never offered to show. If old manuscripts should now be mentioned, I should, unless there were more evidence than can be easily had, suppose them another proof of Scotch conspiracy in national falsehood.

'Do not censure the expression; you know it to be true. . . . .

'I am now engaged, but in a little time I hope to do all you would have. My compliments to Madam and Veronica. I am, Sir, your most humble servant,

'February 7, 1775.'   'SAM. JOHNSON.'

What words were used by Mr. Macpherson in his letter to the venerable Sage, I have never heard; but they are generally said to have been of a nature very different from the language of literary contest. Dr. Johnson's answer appeared in the news-papers of the day, and has since been frequently re-published; but not with perfect accuracy. I give it as dictated to me by himself, written down in his presence, and authenticated by a note in his own hand-writing, '*This, I think, is a true copy*[1].'

'MR. JAMES MACPHERSON,—I received your foolish and impudent letter. Any violence offered me I shall do my best to repel; and what I cannot do for myself, the law shall do for me. I hope I shall never be deterred from detecting what I think a cheat, by the menaces of a ruffian.

'What would you have me retract? I thought your

[1] I have deposited it in the British Museum.

book an imposture; I think it an imposture still. For
this opinion I have given my reasons to the publick,
which I here dare you to refute. Your rage I defy.
Your abilities, since your Homer, are not so formid-
able; and what I hear of your morals inclines me to
pay regard not to what you shall say, but to what
you shall prove. You may print this if you will.

'SAM. JOHNSON.'

83. *Scotchmen and Irishmen* [1775].

His intimacy with many gentlemen of Scotland, and
his employing so many natives of that country as his
amanuenses, prove that his prejudice was not virulent;
and I have deposited in the British Museum, amongst
other pieces of his writing, the following note in
answer to one from me, asking if he would meet
me at dinner at the Mitre, though a friend of mine,
a Scotchman, was to be there:—

'Mr. Johnson does not see why Mr. Boswell should
suppose a Scotchman less acceptable than any other
man. He will be at the Mitre.'

My much-valued friend Dr. Barnard, now Bishop
of Killaloe, having once expressed to him an apprehension, that if he should visit Ireland he might treat
the people of that country more unfavourably than
he had done the Scotch, he answered, with strong
pointed doubled-edged wit, 'Sir, you have no reason
to be afraid of me. The Irish are not in a conspiracy
to cheat the world by false representations of the
merits of their countrymen. No, Sir; the Irish are a
FAIR PEOPLE;—they never speak well of one another.'

84. *Getting Money* [1775].

Mr. Strahan put Johnson in mind of a remark which he had made to him; 'There are few ways in which a man can be more innocently employed than in getting money.' 'The more one thinks of this, (said Strahan,) the juster it will appear.'

85. *Gray* [1775].

Next day I dined with Johnson at Mr. Thrale's. He attacked Gray, calling him 'a dull fellow.' BOSWELL. 'I understand he was reserved, and might appear dull in company; but surely he was not dull in poetry.' JOHNSON. 'Sir, he was dull in company, dull in his closet, dull every where. He was dull in a new way, and that made many people think him GREAT. He was a mechanical poet.' He then repeated some ludicrous lines, which have escaped my memory, and said, 'Is not that GREAT, like his Odes?' Mrs. Thrale maintained that his Odes were melodious; upon which he exclaimed,

　　'Weave the warp, and weave the woof;'—

I added, in a solemn tone,

　　'The winding-sheet of Edward's race.'

'*There* is a good line.' 'Ay, (said he,) and the next line is a good one,' (pronouncing it contemptuously;)

　　'Give ample verge and room enough.'—

'No, Sir, there are but two good stanzas in Gray's poetry, which are in his *Elegy in a Country Church-yard.*' He then repeated the stanza,

　　'For who to dumb forgetfulness a prey,' &c.

mistaking one word; for instead of *precincts* he said *confines.* He added, 'The other stanza I forget.'

86. *Orange Peel* [1775].

Next morning I won a small bet from Lady Diana Beauclerk, by asking him as to one of his particularities, which her Ladyship laid I durst not do. It seems he had been frequently observed at the Club to put into his pocket the Seville oranges, after he had squeezed the juice of them into the drink which he made for himself. Beauclerk and Garrick talked of it to me, and seemed to think that he had a strange unwillingness to be discovered. We could not divine what he did with them; and this was the bold question to be put. I saw on his table the spoils of the preceding night, some fresh peels nicely scraped and cut into pieces. 'O, Sir, (said I,) I now partly see what you do with the squeezed oranges which you put into your pocket at the Club.' JOHNSON. 'I have a great love for them.' BOSWELL. 'And pray, Sir, what do you do with them? You scrape them, it seems, very neatly, and what next?' JOHNSON. 'Let them dry, Sir.' BOSWELL. 'And what next?' JOHNSON. 'Nay, Sir, you shall know their fate no further.' BOSWELL. 'Then the world must be left in the dark. It must be said (assuming a mock solemnity,) he scraped them, and let them dry, but what he did with them next, he never could be prevailed upon to tell.' JOHNSON. 'Nay, Sir, you should say it more emphatically:—he could not be prevailed upon, even by his dearest friends, to tell.'

87. *Doctor of Civil Law* [1775].

He had this morning received his Diploma as Doctor of Laws from the University of Oxford. He did not vaunt of his new dignity, but I understood he was highly pleased with it. I shall here insert the progress and completion of that high academical honour, in the same manner as I have traced his obtaining that of Master of Arts.

To the Reverend Dr. FOTHERGILL, *Vice-Chancellor of the University of* Oxford, *to be communicated to the Heads of Houses, and proposed in Convocation.*

' MR. VICE-CHANCELLOR AND GENTLEMEN,

'THE honour of the degree of M.A. by diploma, formerly conferred upon MR. SAMUEL JOHNSON, in consequence of his having eminently distinguished himself by the publication of a series of Essays, excellently calculated to form the manners of the people, and in which the cause of religion and morality has been maintained and recommended by the strongest powers of argument and elegance of language, reflected an equal degree of lustre upon the University itself.

'The many learned labours which have since that time employed the attention and displayed the abilities of that great man, so much to the advancement of literature and the benefit of the community, render him worthy of more distinguished honours in the Republick of letters: and I persuade myself, that I shall act agreeably to the sentiments of the whole University, in desiring that it may be proposed in Convocation to confer on him the degree of Doctor

in Civil Law by diploma, to which I readily give
my consent; and am, Mr. Vice-Chancellor and Gentlemen, your affectionate friend and servant,

'Downing-street, March 23, 1775.'   'NORTH.'

88. *Nobleness of Resolution* [1775].

I visited him by appointment in the evening, and
we drank tea with Mrs. Williams. He told me that he
had been in the company of a gentleman·whose extraordinary travels had been much the subject of conversation. But I found that he had not listened to him
with that full confidence, without which there is little
satisfaction in the society of travellers. I was curious
to hear what opinion so able a judge as Johnson had
formed of his abilities, and I asked if he was not
a man of sense. JOHNSON. 'Why, Sir, he is not
a distinct relater; and I should say, he is neither
abounding nor deficient in sense. I did not perceive
any superiority of understanding.' BOSWELL. 'But
will you not allow him a nobleness of resolution, in
penetrating into distant regions?' JOHNSON. 'That
Sir, is not to the present purpose. We are talking of
his sense. A fighting cock has a nobleness of resolution.'

89. *Charles II: William III* [1775].

. . . . BOSWELL. 'Sir, it may not be like a gentleman, but it may be genteel.' JOHNSON. 'You are
meaning two different things. One means exteriour
grace; the other honour. It is certain that a man
may be very immoral with exteriour grace. Lovelace,
in *Clarissa*, is a very genteel and a very wicked

character. Tom Hervey, who died t'other day, though a vicious man, was one of the genteelest men that ever lived.' Tom Davies instanced Charles the Second. JOHNSON, (taking fire at any attack upon that Prince, for whom he had an extraordinary partiality,) 'Charles the Second was licentious in his practice; but he always had a reverence for what was good. Charles the Second knew his people, and rewarded merit. The Church was at no time better filled than in his reign. He was the best King we have had from his time till the reign of his present Majesty, except James the Second, who was a very good King, but unhappily believed that it was necessary for the salvation of his subjects that they should be Roman Catholicks. *He* had the merit of endeavouring to do what he thought was for the salvation of the souls of his subjects, till he lost a great Empire. *We*, who thought that we should *not* be saved if we were Roman Catholicks, had the merit of maintaining our religion, at the expence of submitting ourselves to the government of King William, (for it could not be done otherwise,) —to the government of one of the most worthless scoundrels that ever existed. No; Charles the Second was not such as man as——, (naming another King). He did not destroy his father's will. He took money, indeed, from France: but he did not betray those over whom he ruled: He did not let the French fleet pass ours. George the First knew nothing, and desired to know nothing; did nothing, and desired to do nothing: and the only good thing that is told of him is, that he wished to restore the crown to its hereditary successor.' He roared with prodigious violence against George the Second. When he ceased, Moody interjected, in an Irish tone, and with a comick look, 'Ah! poor George the Second.'

90. *Books of Travel* [1775].

Friday, April 7, I dined with him at a Tavern, with a numerous company. JOHNSON. 'I have been reading Twiss's *Travels in Spain*, which are just come out. They are as good as the first book of travels that you will take up. They are as good as those of Keysler or Blainville; nay, as Addison's, if you except the learning. They are not so good as Brydone's, but they are better than Pococke's. I have not, indeed, cut the leaves yet; but I have read in them where the pages are open, and I do not suppose that what is in the pages which are closed is worse than what is in the open pages.'

91. *Domestick Satisfaction* [1775].

No more of his conversation for some days appears in my journal, except that when a gentleman told him he had bought a suit of lace for his lady, he said, 'Well, Sir, you have done a good thing and a wise thing.' 'I have done a good thing, (said the gentleman,) but I do not know that I have done a wise thing.' JOHNSON. 'Yes, Sir; no money is better spent than what is laid out for domestick satisfaction. A man is pleased that his wife is drest as well as other people; and a wife is pleased that she is drest.'

92. *Lord Bute* [1775].

'Lord Bute shewed an undue partiality to Scotchmen. He turned out Dr. Nichols, a very eminent man, from being physician to the King, to make room for one of his countrymen, a man very low in his profession. He had ********** and **** to go on errands for him. He had occasion for people to go on errands for him; but he should not have had Scotchmen; and, certainly, he should not have suffered them to have access to him before the first people in England.'

93. *Hemming Ruffles* [1775].

He observed, 'All knowledge is of itself of some value. There is nothing so minute or inconsiderable, that I would not rather know it than not. In the same manner, all power, of whatever sort, is of itself desirable. A man would not submit to learn to hem a ruffle, of his wife, or his wife's maid; but if a mere wish could attain it, he would rather wish to be able to hem a ruffle.'

94. *Hell Paved with Good Intentions* [1775].

He was pleased to say, 'If you come to settle here, we will have one day in the week on which we will meet by ourselves. That is the happiest conversation where there is no competition, no vanity, but a calm quiet interchange of sentiments.' In his private register this evening is thus marked, 'Boswell sat with me till night; we had some serious talk.' It also appears from the same record, that after I left him he was occupied in religious duties, in 'giving

Francis, his servant, some directions for preparation to communicate; in reviewing his life, and resolving on better conduct.' The humility and piety which he discovers on such occasions, is truely edifying. No saint, however, in the course of his religious warfare, was more sensible of the unhappy failure of pious resolves, than Johnson. He said one day, talking to an acquaintance on this subject, ' Sir, Hell is paved with good intentions[1].'

95. *Advantages of Reading* [1775].

He then took occasion to enlarge on the advantages of reading, and combated the idle superficial notion, that knowledge enough may be acquired in conversation. 'The foundation (said he,) must be laid by reading. General principles must be had from books, which, however, must be brought to the test of real life. In conversation you never get a system. What is said upon a subject is to be gathered from a hundred people. The parts of a truth, which a man gets thus, are at such a distance from each other that he never attains to a full view.'

96. *Polite Learning in Scotland* [1775].

I had brought with me a great bundle of Scotch magazines and news-papers, in which his *Journey to the Western Islands* was attacked in every mode; and I read a great part of them to him, knowing

---

[1] This is a proverbial sentence. ' Hell,' says Herbert, ' is full of good meanings and wishings.' *Jacula Prudentum*, p. 11, edit. 1651. [M.]

they would afford him entertainment. I wish the writers of them had been present: they would have been sufficiently vexed. One ludicrous imitation of his style, by Mr. Maclaurin, now one of the Scotch Judges, with the title of Lord Dreghorn, was distinguished by him from the rude mass. 'This (said he,) is the best. But I could caricature my own style much better myself.' He defended his remark upon the general insufficiency of education in Scotland; and confirmed to me the authenticity of his witty saying on the learning of the Scotch;—'Their learning is like bread in a besieged town: every man gets a little, but no man gets a full meal.' 'There is (said he,) in Scotland a diffusion of learning, a certain portion of it widely and thinly spread. A merchant there has as much learning as one of their clergy.'

97. *The Backs of Books* [1775].

No sooner had we made our bow to Mr. Cambridge, in his library, than Johnson ran eagerly to one side of the room, intent on poring over the backs of the books. Sir Joshua observed, (aside,) 'He runs to the books, as I do to the pictures: but I have the advantage. I can see much more of the pictures than he can of the books.' Mr. Cambridge, upon this, politely said, 'Dr. Johnson, I am going, with your pardon, to accuse myself, for I have the same custom which I perceive you have. But it seems odd that one should have such a desire to look at the backs of books.' Johnson, ever ready for contest, instantly started from his reverie, wheeled about, and answered,

'Sir, the reason is very plain. Knowledge is of two kinds. We know a subject ourselves, or we know where we can find information upon it. When we enquire into any subject, the first thing we have to do is to know what books have treated of it. This leads us to look at catalogues, and the backs of books in libraries.' Sir Joshua observed to me the extraordinary promptitude with which Johnson flew upon an argument. 'Yes, (said I,) he has no formal preparation, no flourishing with his sword; he is through your body in an instant.'

98. *Scotch Oat-cakes and Scotch Prejudices* [1775. *Letter to Boswell*].

'Make my compliments to Mrs. Boswell, though she does not love me. You see what perverse things ladies are, and how little fit to be trusted with feudal estates. When she mends and loves me, there may be more hope of her daughters.

'I will not send compliments to my friends by name, because I would be loath to leave any out in the enumeration. Tell them, as you see them, how well I speak of Scotch politeness, and Scotch hospitality, and Scotch beauty, and of every thing Scotch, but Scotch oat-cakes, and Scotch prejudices.'

99. *The State of Life* [1775. *Letter to Boswell*].

'DEAR SIR,—I am returned from the annual ramble into the middle counties. Having seen nothing I had not seen before, I have nothing to relate. Time has left that part of the island few antiquities; and commerce has left the people no singularities. I was glad to go abroad, and, perhaps, glad to come home; which is, in other words, I was, I am afraid, weary of being at home, and weary of being abroad. Is not this the state of life? But, if we confess this weariness, let us not lament it; for all the wise and all the good say, that we may cure it.'

100. *Melancholy* [1776].

Talking of constitutional melancholy, he observed, 'A man so afflicted, Sir, must divert distressing thoughts, and not combat with them.' BOSWELL. 'May not he think them down, Sir?' JOHNSON. 'No, Sir. To attempt to *think them down* is madness. He should have a lamp constantly burning in his bed-chamber during the night, and if wakefully disturbed, take a book, and read, and compose himself to rest. 'To have the management of the mind is a great art, and it may be attained in a considerable degree by experience and habitual exercise.' BOSWELL. 'Should not he provide amusements for himself? Would it not, for instance, be right for him to take a course of chymistry?' JOHNSON. 'Let him take a course of chymistry, or a course of rope-dancing, or a course of any thing to which he is inclined at the time. Let him contrive to have as many retreats for his mind as he can, as many things to which it can fly from itself. Burton's *Anatomy of Melancholy* is a valuable work. It is, perhaps, overloaded with quotation. But there is great spirit and great power in what Burton says, when he writes from his own mind.'

H 2

101. *Biography* [1776].

We then went to Trinity College, where he introduced me to Mr. Thomas Warton, with whom we
passed a part of the evening. We talked of biography.
—JOHNSON. 'It is rarely well executed. They only
who live with a man can write his life with any
genuine exactness and discrimination; and few people
who have lived with a man know what to remark
about him. The chaplain of a late Bishop, whom
I was to assist in writing some memoirs of his Lordship, could tell me scarcely any thing.'

102. *Getting Information* [1776].

Mr. Warton, being engaged, could not sup with
us at our inn; we had therefore another evening by
ourselves. I asked Johnson, whether a man's being
forward to make himself known to eminent people,
and seeing as much of life, and getting as much information as he could in every way, was not yet
lessening himself by his forwardness. JOHNSON. 'No,
Sir; a man always makes himself greater as he
increases his knowledge.'

103. *Taverns* [1776].

Sir John Hawkins has preserved very few *Memora-
bilia* of Johnson. There is, however, to be found, in
his bulky tome [p. 87], a very excellent one upon this
subject:—' In contradiction to those, who, having a wife
and children, prefer domestick enjoyments to those
which a tavern affords, I have heard him assert, *that
a tavern chair was the throne of human felicity.*—

"As soon," said he, "as I enter the door of a tavern, I experience an oblivion of care, and a freedom from solicitude: when I am seated, I find the master courteous, and the servants obsequious to my call; anxious to know and ready to supply my wants: wine there exhilarates my spirit, and prompts me to free conversation and an interchange of discourse with those whom I most love: I dogmatise and am contradicted, and in this conflict of opinions and sentiments I find delight."

104. *The Grey Rat* [1776].

I told him, that I heard Dr. Percy was writing the history of the wolf in Great-Britain. JOHNSON. 'The wolf, Sir! why the wolf? Why does he not write of the bear, which we had formerly? Nay, it is said we had the beaver. Or why does he not write of the grey rat, the Hanover rat, as it is called, because it is said to have come into this country about the time that the family of Hanover came? I should like to see *The History of the Grey Rat, by Thomas Percy, D.D. Chaplain in Ordinary to His Majesty,'* (laughing immoderately). BOSWELL. 'I am afraid a court chaplain could not decently write of the grey rat.' JOHNSON. 'Sir, he need not give it the name of the Hanover rat.' Thus could he indulge a luxuriant sportive imagination, when talking of a friend whom he loved and esteemed.

105. *Marriage* [1776].

BOSWELL. 'Pray, Sir, do you not suppose that there are fifty women in the world, with any one of whom a man may be as happy, as with any one woman in particular? JOHNSON. 'Ay, Sir, fifty thousand.' BOSWELL. 'Then, Sir, you are not of opinion with some who imagine that certain men and certain women are made for each other; and that they cannot be happy if they miss their counterparts?' JOHNSON. 'To be sure not, Sir. I believe marriages would in general be as happy, and often more so, if they were all made by the Lord Chancellor, upon a due consideration of characters and circumstances, without the parties having any choice in the matter.'

106. *Vexing Thoughts* [1776].

Talking of melancholy, he said, 'Some men, and very thinking men too, have not those vexing thoughts. Sir Joshua Reynolds is the same all the year round. Beauclerk, except when ill and in pain, is the same. But I believe most men have them in the degree in which they are capable of having them. If I were in the country, and were distressed by that malady, I would force myself to take a book; and every time I did it I should find it the easier. Melancholy, indeed, should be diverted by every means but drinking.'

107. *Whole Libraries* [1776].

On Wednesday, April 3, in the morning I found him very busy putting his books in order, and as they were generally very old ones, clouds of dust were flying around him. He had on a pair of large gloves such as hedgers use. His present appearance put me in mind of my uncle, Dr. Boswell's description of him, 'A robust genius, born to grapple with whole libraries.'

108. *Omai* [1776].

He had been in company with Omai, a native of one of the South Sea Islands, after he had been some time in this country. He was struck with the elegance of his behaviour, and accounted for it thus: ' Sir, he had passed his time, while in England, only in the best company; so that all that he had acquired of our manners was genteel. As a proof of this, Sir, Lord Mulgrave and he dined one day at Streatham; they sat with their backs to the light fronting me, so that I could not see distinctly ; and there was so little of the savage in Omai, that I was afraid to speak to either, lest I should mistake one for the other.'

109. *The Character of a Soldier* [1776].

'The character of a soldier is high. They who stand forth the foremost in danger, for the community, have the respect of mankind. An officer is much more respected than any other man who has as little money. In a commercial country, money will always purchase respect. But you find, an officer, who has, properly speaking, no money, is every where well received and treated with attention. The character of a soldier always stands him in stead.' BOSWELL. ' Yet, Sir, I think that common soldiers are worse thought of than other men in the same rank of life; such as labourers.' JOHNSON. ' Why, Sir, a common soldier is usually a very gross man, and any quality which procures respect may be overwhelmed by grossness. A man of learning may be so vicious or so ridiculous that you cannot respect him. A common soldier too, generally eats more than he can pay for. But when a common soldier is civil in his quarters, his red coat procures him a degree of respect.'

110. *Mutilated Editions* [1776].

Mr. Murphy mentioned Dr. Johnson's having a design to publish an edition of Cowley. Johnson said, he did not know but he should; and he expressed his disapprobation of Dr. Hurd, for having published a mutilated edition under the title of *Select Works of Abraham Cowley.* Mr. Murphy thought it a bad precedent; observing, that any authour might be used in the same manner; and that it was pleasing to see the variety of an authour's compositions, at different periods.

We talked of Flatman's Poems; and Mrs. Thrale observed, that Pope had partly borrowed from him, *The dying Christian to his Soul.* Johnson repeated Rochester's verses upon Flatman, which I think by much too severe:

'Nor that slow drudge in swift Pindarick strains,
Flatman, who Cowley imitates with pains,
And rides a jaded Muse, whipt with loose reins.'

I like to recollect all the passages that I heard Johnson repeat: it stamps a value on them.

111. *The Reviews* [1776].

'The Critical Reviewers, I believe, often review without reading the books through; but lay hold of a topick, and write chiefly from their own minds. The Monthly Reviewers are duller men, and are glad to read the books through.'

112. *The Mediterranean* [1776].

A journey to Italy was still in his thoughts. He said, 'A man who has not been in Italy, is always conscious of an inferiority, from his not having seen what it is expected a man should see. The grand object of travelling is to see the shores of the Mediterranean. On those shores were the four great Empires of the world; the Assyrian, the Persian, the Grecian, and the Roman.—All our religion, almost all our law, almost all our arts, almost all that sets us above savages, has come to us from the shores of the Mediterranean.' The General [Paoli] observed, that 'THE MEDITERRANEAN would be a noble subject for a poem.'

113. *Translation* [1776].

We talked of translation. I said, I could not define it, nor could I think of a similitude to illustrate it; but that it appeared to me the translation of poetry could be only imitation. JOHNSON. 'You may translate books of science exactly. You may also translate history, in so far as it is not embellished with oratory, which is poetical. Poetry, indeed, cannot be translated; and, therefore, it is the poets that preserve languages; for we would not be at the trouble to learn a language, if we could have all that is written in it just as well in a translation. But as the beauties of poetry cannot be preserved in any language except that in which it was originally written, we learn the language.'

114. *Poetry* [1776].

I related a dispute between Goldsmith and Mr. Robert Dodsley, one day when they and I were dining

at Tom Davies's, in 1762. Goldsmith asserted, that
there was no poetry produced in this age. Dodsley
appealed to his own *Collection*, and maintained, that
though you could not find a palace like Dryden's *Ode
on St. Cecilia's Day*, you had villages composed of
very pretty houses; and he mentioned particularly
The Spleen. JOHNSON. ' I think Dodsley gave up the
question. He and Goldsmith said the same thing;
only he said it in a softer manner than Goldsmith did;
for he acknowledged that there was no poetry, nothing
that towered above the common mark. You may
find wit and humour in verse, and yet no poetry.
Hudibras has a profusion of these; yet it is not to be
reckoned a poem. *The Spleen*, in Dodsley's *Collection*,
on which you say he chiefly rested, is not poetry.'
BOSWELL. 'Does not Gray's poetry, Sir, tower
above the common mark?' JOHNSON. 'Yes, Sir; but
we must attend to the difference between what men in
general cannot do if they would, and what every man
may do if he would. Sixteen-string Jack[1] towered
above the common mark.' BOSWELL. Then, Sir, what
is poetry?' JOHNSON. 'Why, Sir, it is much easier
to say what it is not. We all *know* what light is;
but it is not easy to *tell* what it is.'

115. *Reading with Inclination* [1776].

He told us, 'almost all his *Ramblers* were written
just as they were wanted for the press; that he sent a

---

[1] A noted highwayman, who after having been several times
tried and acquitted, was at last hanged. He was remarkable
for foppery in his dress, and particularly for wearing a bunch of
sixteen strings at the knees of his breeches.

certain portion of the copy of an essay, and wrote the remainder, while the former part of it was printing. When it was wanted, and he had fairly sat down to it, he was sure it would be done.'

He said, that for general improvement, a man should read whatever his immediate inclination prompts him to; though, to be sure, if a man has a science to learn, he must regularly and resolutely advance. He added, 'what we read with inclination makes a much stronger impression. If we read without inclination, half the mind is employed in fixing the attention; so there is but one half to be employed on what we read.' He told us, he read Fielding's *Amelia* through without stopping. He said, 'if a man begins to read in the middle of a book, and feels an inclination to go on, let him not quit it, to go to the beginning. He may perhaps not feel again the inclination.'

116. *Writing for Money* [1776].

We talked of the Reviews, and Dr. Johnson spoke of them as he did at Thrale's. Sir Joshua said, what I have often thought, that he wondered to find so much good writing employed in them, when the authours were to remain unknown, and so could not have the motive of fame. JOHNSON. 'Nay, Sir, those who write in them, write well, in order to be paid well.'

117. *Chatterton* [1776].

On Monday, April 29, he and I made an excursion to Bristol, where I was entertained with seeing him enquire upon the spot, into the authenticity of 'Rowley's Poetry,' as I had seen him enquire upon the spot into the authenticity of 'Ossian's Poetry.' George Catcot, the pewterer, who was as zealous for Rowley, as Dr. Hugh Blair was for Ossian, (I trust my Reverend friend will excuse the comparison,) attended us at our inn, and with a triumphant air of lively simplicity called out, 'I'll make Dr. Johnson a convert.' Dr. Johnson, at his desire, read aloud some of Chatterton's fabricated verses, while Catcot stood at the back of his chair, moving himself like a pendulum, and beating time with his feet, and now and then looking into Dr. Johnson's face, wondering that he was not yet convinced. We called on Mr. Barret, the surgeon, and saw some of the *originals* as they were called, which were executed very artificially; but from a careful inspection of them, and a consideration of the circumstances with which they were attended, we were quite satisfied of the imposture, which, indeed, has been clearly demonstrated from internal evidence, by several able criticks[1].' . . . ..

Johnson said of Chatterton, 'This is the most extraordinary young man that has encountered my knowledge. It is wonderful how the whelp has written such things.'

118. *You have but two topicks* [1776].

Being irritated by hearing a gentleman ask Mr. Levett a variety of questions concerning him, when he was sitting by, he broke out, 'Sir, you have but two topicks, yourself and me. I am sick of both.' 'A man, (said he,) should not talk of himself, nor much of any

---

[1] Mr. Tyrwhitt, Mr. Warton, Mr. Malone.

particular person. He should take care not to be
made a proverb; and, therefore, should avoid having
any one topick of which people can say, " We shall
hear him upon it." '

119. *The Liberty of the Pulpit* [1776].

During my stay in London this spring, I solicited
his attention to another law case, in which I was
engaged. In the course of a contested election for the
Borough of Dumfermline, which I attended as one of
my friend Colonel (afterwards Sir Archibald) Campbell's counsel; one of his political agents, who was
charged with having been unfaithful to his employer,
and having deserted to the opposite party for a pecu-
niary reward—attacked very rudely in a news-paper
the Reverend Mr. James Thomson, one of the ministers
of that place, on account of a supposed allusion to him
in one of his sermons. Upon this the minister, on a
subsequent Sunday, arraigned him by name from the
pulpit with some severity ; and the agent, after the ser-
mon was over, rose up and asked the minister aloud,
'What bribe he had received for telling so many lies
from the chair of verity.' I was present at this very
extraordinary scene. The person arraigned, and his
father and brother, who had also had a share both
of the reproof from the pulpit, and in the retaliation,
brought an action against Mr. Thomson, in the Court
of Session, for defamation and damages, and I was one
of the counsel for the reverend defendant. The *Liberty
of the Pulpit* was our great ground of defence ; but we
argued also on the provocation of the previous attack,

and on the instant retaliation. The Court of Session, however—the fifteen Judges, who are at the same time the Jury, decided against the minister, contrary to my humble opinion ; and several of them expressed themselves with indignation against him. He was an aged gentleman, formerly a military chaplain, and a man of high spirit and honour. Johnson was satisfied that the judgement was wrong, and dictated to me the following argument in confutation of it :

'Of the censure pronounced from the pulpit, our determination must be formed, as in other cases, by a consideration of the action itself, and the particular circumstances with which it is invested.

'The right of censure and rebuke seems necessarily appendant to the pastoral office. He, to whom the care of a congregation is entrusted, is considered as the shepherd of a flock, as the teacher of a school, as the father of a family. As a shepherd tending not his own sheep but those of his master, he is answerable for those that stray, and that lose themselves by straying. But no man can be answerable for losses which he has not power to prevent, or for vagrancy which he has not authority to restrain.

'As a teacher giving instruction for wages, and liable to reproach, if those whom he undertakes to inform make no proficiency, he must have the power of enforcing attendance, of awakening negligence, and repressing contradiction.

'As a father, he possesses the paternal authority of admonition, rebuke, and punishment. He cannot, without reducing his office to an empty name, be hindered from the exercise of any practice necessary to stimulate the idle, to reform the vicious, to check the petulant, and correct the stubborn.

'If we enquire into the practice of the primitive church, we shall, I believe, find the ministers of the word, exercising the whole authority of this complicated character. We shall find them not only encouraging the good by exhortation, but terrifying the wicked by reproof and denunciation. In the earliest ages of the Church, while religion was yet pure from secular advantages, the punishment of sinners was publick censure, and open penance; penalties inflicted merely by ecclesiastical authority, at a time while the Church had yet no help from the civil power; while the hand of the magistrate lifted only the rod of persecution; and when governours were ready to afford a refuge to all those who fled from clerical authority.

'That the Church, therefore, had once a power of publick censure is evident, because that power was frequently exercised. That it borrowed not its power from the civil authority, is likewise certain, because civil authority was at that time its enemy.

'The hour came at length, when after three hundred years of struggle and distress, Truth took possession of imperial power, and the civil laws lent their aid to the ecclesiastical constitutions. The magistrate from that time co-operated with the priest, and clerical sentences were made efficacious by secular force. But the State, when it came to the assistance of the Church, had no intention to diminish its authority. Those rebukes and those censures which were lawful before, were

lawful still.   But they had hitherto operated only upon
voluntary submission.   The refractory and contemptuous were at first in no danger of temporal severities,
except what they might suffer from the reproaches of
conscience, or the detestation of their fellow Christians.
When religion obtained the support of law, if admonitions and censures had no effect, they were seconded by
the magistrates with coercion and punishment.

' It therefore appears from ecclesiastical history, that
the right of inflicting shame by publick censure, has
been always considered as inherent in the Church ; and
that this right was not conferred by the civil power;
for it was exercised when the civil power operated
against it.   By the civil power it was never taken
away ; for the Christian magistrate interposed his
office, not to rescue sinners from censure, but to
supply more powerful means of reformation ; to add
pain where shame was insufficient ; and when men were
proclaimed unworthy of the society of the faithful, to
restrain them by imprisonment, from spreading abroad
the contagion of wickedness.

' It is not improbable that from this acknowledged
power of publick censure, grew in time the practice of
auricular confession.   Those who dreaded the blast of
publick reprehension, were willing to submit themselves to the priest, by a private accusation of themselves ; and to obtain a reconciliation with the Church
by a kind of clandestine absolution and invisible
penance ; conditions with which the priest would in
times of ignorance and corruption, easily comply, as
they increased his influence, by adding the knowledge of

secret sins to that of notorious offences, and enlarged his authority, by making him the sole arbiter of the terms of reconcilement.

'From this bondage the Reformation set us free. The minister has no longer power to press into the retirements of conscience, to torture us by interroga-tories, or put himself in possession of our secrets and our lives. But though we have thus controlled his usurpations, his just and original power remains unimpaired. He may still see, though he may not pry: he may yet hear, though he may not question. And that knowledge which his eyes and ears force upon him it is still his duty to use, for the benefit of his flock. A father who lives near a wicked neighbour, may forbid a son to frequent his company. A minister who has in his congregation a man of open and scandalous wickedness, may warn his parishioners to shun his conversation. To warn them is not only lawful, but not to warn them would be criminal. He may warn them one by one in friendly converse, or by a parochial visitation. But if he may warn each man singly, what shall forbid him to warn them all together? Of that which is to be made known to all, how is there any difference whether it be communicated to each singly, or to all together? What is known to all, must necessarily be publick. Whether it shall be publick at once, or publick by degrees, is the only question. And of a sudden and solemn publication the impression is deeper, and the warning more effectual.

'It may easily be urged, if a minister be thus left at liberty to delate sinners from the pulpit, and to publish

at will the crimes of a parishioner, he may often blast
the innocent, and distress the timorous. He may be
suspicious, and condemn without evidence; he may be
rash, and judge without examination; he may be
severe, and treat slight offences with too much harsh-
ness; he may be malignant and partial, and gratify his
private interest or resentment under the shelter of his
pastoral character.

'Of all this there is possibility, and of all this there
is danger. But if possibility of evil be to exclude
good, no good ever can be done. If nothing is to be
attempted in which there is danger, we must all sink
into hopeless inactivity. The evils that may be feared
from this practice arise not from any defect in the
institution, but from the infirmities of human nature.
Power, in whatever hands it is placed, will be sometimes improperly exerted; yet courts of law must
judge, though they will sometimes judge amiss. A
father must instruct his children, though he himself
may often want instruction. A minister must censure
sinners, though his censure may be sometimes erroneous by want of judgement, and sometimes unjust by
want of honesty.

'If we examine the circumstances of the present case,
we shall find the sentence neither erroneous nor unjust;
we shall find no breach of private confidence, no intrusion into secret transactions. The fact was notorious
and indubitable; so easy to be proved, that no proof
was desired. The act was base and treacherous, the per-
petration insolent and open, and the example naturally
mischievous. The minister however, being retired

and recluse, had not yet heard what was publickly known throughout the parish; and on occasion of a publick election, warned his people, according to his duty, against the crimes which publick elections frequently produce. His warning was felt by one of his parish-ioners, as pointed particularly at himself. But instead of producing, as might be wished, private compunc-tion and immediate reformation, it kindled only rage and resentment. He charged his minister, in a publick paper, with scandal, defamation, and falsehood. The minister, thus reproached, had his own character to vindi-cate, upon which his pastoral authority must necessarily depend. To be charged with a defamatory lie is an injury which no man patiently endures in common life. To be charged with polluting the pastoral office with scandal and falsehood, was a violation of character still more atrocious, as it affected not only his personal but his clerical veracity. His indignation naturally rose in proportion to his honesty, and with all the fortitude of injured honesty, he dared this calumniator in the church, and at once exonerated himself from censure, and rescued his flock from deception and from danger. The man whom he accuses pretends not to be innocent; or at least only pretends; for he declines a trial. The crime of which he is accused has frequent opportunities and strong temptations. It has already spread far, with much depravation of private morals, and much injury to publick happiness. To warn the people, therefore, against it was not wanton and offi-cious, but necessary and pastoral.

'What then is the fault with which this worthy

minister is charged? He has usurped no dominion over conscience. He has exerted no authority in support of doubtful and controverted opinions. He has not dragged into light a bashful and corrigible sinner. His censure was directed against a breach of morality, against an act which no man justifies. The man who appropriated this censure to himself, is evidently and notoriously guilty. His consciousness of his own wickedness incited him to attack his faithful reprover with open insolence and printed accusations. Such an attack made defence necessary; and we hope it will be at last decided that the means of defence were just and lawful.'

120. *Johnson and Wilkes* [1776].

I am now to record a very curious incident in Dr. Johnson's Life, which fell under my own observation; of which *pars magna fui*, and which I am persuaded will, with the liberal-minded, be much to his credit.

My desire of being acquainted with celebrated men of every description, had made me, much about the same time, obtain an introduction to Dr. Samuel Johnson and to John Wilkes, Esq. Two men more different could perhaps not be selected out of all mankind. They had even attacked one another with some asperity in their writings; yet I lived in habits of friendship with both. I could fully relish the excellence of each; for I have ever delighted in that intellectual chymistry, which can separate good qualities from evil in the same person.

Sir John Pringle, 'mine own friend and my Father's friend,' between whom and Dr. Johnson I in vain wished to establish an acquaintance, as I respected and lived in intimacy with both of them, observed to me once, very ingeniously, 'It is not in friendship as in mathematicks, where two things, each equal to a third, are equal between themselves. You agree with Johnson as a middle quality, and you agree with me as a middle quality; but Johnson and I should not agree.' Sir John was not sufficiently flexible; so I desisted; knowing, indeed, that the repulsion was equally strong on the part of Johnson; who, I know not from what cause, unless his being a Scotchman, had formed a very erroneous opinion of Sir John. But I conceived an irresistible wish, if possible, to bring Dr. Johnson and Mr. Wilkes together. How to manage it, was a nice and difficult matter.

My worthy booksellers and friends, Messieurs Dilly in the Poultry, at whose hospitable and well-covered table I have seen a greater number of literary men, than at any other, except that of Sir Joshua Reynolds, had invited me to meet Mr. Wilkes and some more gentlemen on Wednesday, May 15. 'Pray (said I,) let us have Dr. Johnson.'—'What with Mr. Wilkes? not for the world, (said Mr. Edward Dilly :) Dr. Johnson would never forgive me.'—'Come, (said I,) if you'll let me negociate for you, I will be answerable that all shall go well.' DILLY. 'Nay, if you will take it upon you, I am sure I shall be very happy to see them both here.'

Notwithstanding the high veneration which I

entertained for Dr. Johnson, I was sensible that he was
sometimes a little actuated by the spirit of contradiction,
and by means of that I hoped I should gain my point.
I was persuaded that if I had come upon him with a
direct proposal, 'Sir, will you dine in company with
Jack Wilkes?' he would have flown into a passion
and would probably have answered, 'Dine with Jack
Wilkes, Sir! I'd as soon dine with Jack Ketch[1].' I
therefore, while we were sitting quietly by ourselves
at his house in an evening, took occasion to open my
plan thus:—'Mr. Dilly, Sir, sends his respectful
compliments to you, and would be happy if you would
do him the honour to dine with him on Wednesday
next along with me, as I must soon go to Scotland.'
JOHNSON 'Sir, I am obliged to Mr. Dilly. I will wait
upon him—' BOSWELL. 'Provided, Sir, I suppose, that
the company which he is to have, is agreeable to you.'
JOHNSON. 'What do you mean, Sir? What do you
take me for? Do you think I am so ignorant of the
world, as to imagine that I am to prescribe to a gentleman what company he is to have at his table?'
BOSWELL. 'I beg your pardon, Sir, for wishing
to prevent you from meeting people whom you
might not like. Perhaps he may have some of what
he calls his patriotick friends with him.' JOHNSON.
'Well, Sir, and what then? What care *I* for his *patriotick friends*? Poh!' BOSWELL. 'I should not be surprized to find Jack Wilkes there.' JOHNSON. 'And if Jack
Wilkes *should* be there, what is that to *me*, Sir? My

---

[1] This has been circulated as if actually said by Johnson;
when the truth is, it was only *supposed* by me.

dear friend, let us have no more of this. I am sorry to be angry with you; but really it is treating me strangely to talk to me as if I could not meet any company whatever, occasionally.' BOSWELL. 'Pray forgive me, Sir: I meant well. But you shall meet whoever comes, for me.' Thus I secured him, and told Dilly that he would find him very well pleased to be one of his guests on the day appointed.

Upon the much-expected Wednesday, I called on him about half an hour before dinner, as I often did when we were to dine out together, to see that he was ready in time, and to accompany him. I found him buffeting his books, as upon a former occasion, covered with dust, and making no preparation for going abroad. 'How is this, Sir? (said I.) Don't you recollect that you are to dine at Mr. Dilly's?' JOHN-SON. 'Sir, I did not think of going to Dilly's: it went out of my head. I have ordered dinner at home with Mrs. Williams.' BOSWELL. 'But, my dear Sir, you know you were engaged to Mr. Dilly, and I told him so. He will expect you, and will be much disappointed if you don't come.' JOHNSON. 'You must talk to Mrs. Williams about this.'

Here was a sad dilemma. I feared that what I was so confident I had secured would yet be frustrated. He had accustomed himself to shew Mrs. Williams such a degree of humane attention, as frequently imposed some restraint upon him; and I knew that if she should be obstinate, he would not stir. I hastened down stairs to the blind lady's room, and told her I was in great uneasiness, for Dr. Johnson had engaged to me to dine this day at Mr. Dilly's, but that he had told me he had forgotten his engagement, and had ordered dinner at home. 'Yes, Sir, (said she, pretty peevishly,) Dr. Johnson is to dine at home.'—'Madam, (said I,) his respect for you is such, that I know he will not leave you unless you absolutely desire it. But as you have so much of his company, I hope you will be good enough to forego it for a day; as Mr. Dilly is a very worthy man, has frequently had agreeable parties at his house for Dr. Johnson, and will be vexed if the Doctor neglects him to-day. And then, Madam, be pleased to consider my situation; I carried the message, and I assured Mr. Dilly that Dr. Johnson was to come, and no doubt he has made a dinner, and invited a company, and boasted of the honour he expected to have. I shall be quite disgraced if the Doctor is not there.' She gradually softened to my solicitations, which were certainly as earnest as most entreaties to ladies upon any occasion, and was graciously pleased to empower me to tell Dr. Johnson, 'That all things considered, she thought he should certainly go.' I flew back to him, still in dust, and careless of what should be the event, 'indifferent in his choice to go or stay;' but as soon as I had announced to him Mrs. Williams' consent, he roared, 'Frank, a clean shirt,' and was very soon drest. When I had him fairly seated in a hackney-coach with me, I exulted as much as a fortune-hunter who has got an heiress into a post-chaise with him to set out for Gretna-Green.

When we entered Mr. Dilly's drawing room, he found himself in the midst of a company he did not know. I kept myself snug and silent, watching how he would conduct himself. I observed him whispering to Mr. Dilly, 'Who is that gentleman, Sir?'—'Mr. Arthur Lee.'—JOHNSON. 'Too, too, too,' (under his breath,) which was one of his habitual mutterings. Mr. Arthur Lee could not but be very obnoxious to Johnson, for he was not only a *patriot* but an *American*. He was afterwards minister from the United States at the court of Madrid. 'And who is the gentleman in lace?'—'Mr. Wilkes, Sir.' This information confounded him still more: he had some difficulty to restrain himself, and taking up a book, sat down upon a window-seat and read, or at least kept his eye upon it intently for some time, till he composed himself. His feelings, I dare say, were aukward enough. But he no doubt recollected his having rated me for supposing that he could be at all disconcerted by any company, and he, therefore, resolutely set himself to behave quite as an easy man of the world, who could adapt himself at once to the disposition and manners of those whom he might chance to meet.

The cheering sound of 'Dinner is upon the table,' dissolved his reverie, and we *all* sat down without any symptom of ill humour. There were present, beside Mr. Wilkes, and Mr. Arthur Lee, who was an old companion of mine when he studied physick at Edinburgh, Mr. (now Sir John) Miller, Dr. Lettsom, and Mr. Slater the druggist. Mr. Wilkes placed himself next to Dr. Johnson, and behaved to him with so much attention and politeness, that he gained upon him insensibly. No man eat more heartily than

Johnson, or loved better what was nice and delicate. Mr. Wilkes was very assiduous in helping him to some fine veal. 'Pray give me leave, Sir:—It is better here— A little of the brown—Some fat, Sir—A little of the stuffing—Some gravy—Let me have the pleasure of giving you some butter—Allow me to recommend a squeeze of this orange;—or the lemon, perhaps, may have more zest.'—'Sir, Sir, I am obliged to you, Sir,' cried Johnson, bowing, and turning his head to him with a look for some time of 'surly virtue [1],' but, in a short while, of complacency.

121. *Dryden and Cibber* [1776].

Talking of the great difficulty of obtaining authentick information for biography, Johnson told us, 'When I was a young fellow I wanted to write the *Life of Dryden*, and in order to get materials, I applied to the only two persons then alive who had seen him; these were old Swinney, and old Cibber. Swinney's information was no more than this, "That at Will's coffee-house Dryden had a particular chair for himself, which was set by the fire in winter, and was then called his winter-chair; and that it was carried out for him to the balcony in summer, and was then called his summer-chair." Cibber could tell no more but "That he remembered him a decent old man, arbiter of critical disputes at Will's." You are to consider that Cibber was then at a great distance from Dryden, had perhaps one leg only in the room, and durst not draw in the other.'

[1] Johnson's *London, a Poem*, v. 145.

122. *Goldsmith's Epitaph* [1776].

It was, I think, after I had left London this year, that this Epitaph gave occasion to a *Remonstrance* to the MONARCH OF LITERATURE, for an account of which I am indebted to Sir William Forbes, of Pitsligo.

That my readers may have the subject more fully and clearly before them, I shall first insert the Epitaph.

> OLIVARII GOLDSMITH,
> *Poetæ, Physici, Historici,*
> *Qui nullum ferè scribendi genus*
> *Non tetigit,*
> *Nullum quod tetigit non ornavit:*
> *Sive risus essent movendi,*
> *Sive lacrymæ,*
> *Affectuum potens at lenis dominator:*
> *Ingenio sublimis, vividus, versatilis,*
> *Oratione grandis, nitidus, venustus:*
> *Hoc monumento memoriam coluit*
> *Sodalium amor,*
> *Amicorum fides,*
> *Lectorum veneratio.*
> *Natus in Hiberniâ Forniæ Longfordiensis,*
> *In loco cui nomen Pallas,*
> *Nov.* XXIX. MDCCXXXI ;
> *Eblanæ literis institutus;*
> *Obiit Londini,*
> *April* IV, MDCCLXXIV.'

Sir William Forbes writes to me thus :

' I enclose the *Round Robin.* This *jeu d'esprit* took its rise one day at dinner at our friend Sir Joshua Reynolds's. All the company present, except myself, were friends and acquaintance of Dr. Goldsmith. The Epitaph, written for him by Dr. Johnson, became the subject of conversation, and various emendations were suggested, which it was agreed should be submitted to the Doctor's consideration.—But the question was, who should have the courage to propose them to him? At last it was hinted, that there could be no way so good as that of a *Round Robin*, as the sailors call it, which they make use of when they enter into a conspiracy, so as not to let it be known who puts his name first or last to the paper. This proposition was instantly assented to; and Dr. Barnard, Dean of Derry, now Bishop of Killaloe, drew up an address to Dr. Johnson on the occasion, replete with wit and humour, but which it was feared the Doctor might think treated the subject with too much levity. Mr. Burke then proposed the address as it stands in the paper in writing, to which I had the honour to officiate as clerk.

'Sir Joshua agreed to carry it to Dr. Johnson, who received it with much good humour [1], and desired Sir Joshua to tell the gentlemen, that he would alter the Epitaph in any manner they pleased, as to the sense of it; but *he would never consent to disgrace the walls of Westminster Abbey with an English inscription.*

'I consider this *Round Robin* as a species of literary curiosity worth preserving, as it marks, in a certain degree, Dr. Johnson's character.'

My readers are presented with a faithful transcript

---

[1] ... Applying to Goldsmith equally the epithets of '*Poetæ, Historici, Physici*,' is surely not right; for as to his claim to the last of those epithets, I have heard Johnson himself say, 'Goldsmith, Sir, will give us a very fine book upon the subject; but if he can distinguish a cow from a horse, that, I believe, may be the extent of his knowledge of natural history.'

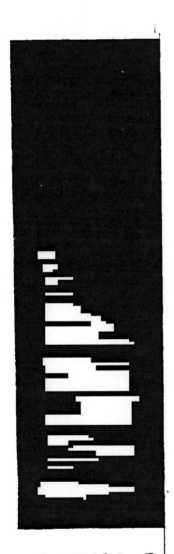

ROUND R

of a paper, which I doubt not of their being desirous
to see.

Sir William Forbes's observation is very just. The
anecdote now related proves, in the strongest manner,
the reverence and awe with which Johnson was regarded, by some of the most eminent men of his time, in
various departments, and even by such of them as lived
most with him; while it also confirms what I have
again and again inculcated, that he was by no means
of that ferocious and irascible character which has been
ignorantly imagined.

This hasty composition is also to be remarked as one
of a thousand instances which evince the extraordinary
promptitude of Mr. Burke; who while he is equal to
the greatest things, can adorn the least; can, with
equal facility, embrace the vast and complicated
speculations of politicks, or the ingenious topicks of
literary investigation.

123. *Sir Alexander Dick to Dr. Samuel Johnson*
[1777].

'SIR,   'Prestonfield, Feb. 17, 1777.

'I had yesterday the honour of receiving your
book of your *Journey to the Western Islands of Scotland*, which you was so good as to send me, by the
hands of our mutual friend, Mr. Boswell, of Auchinleck;
for which I return you my most hearty thanks; and
after carefully reading it over again, shall deposit in
my little collection of choice books, next our worthy
friend's *Journey to Corsica*, as there are many things

to admire in both performances. I have often wished
that no Travels or Journeys should be published but
those undertaken by persons of integrity and capacity,
to judge well, and describe faithfully, and in good
language, the situation, condition, and manners of the
countries past through.   Indeed our country of Scotland, in spite of the union of the crowns, is still in
most places so devoid of clothing, or cover from hedges
and plantations, that it was well you gave your readers
a sound *Monitoire* with respect to that circumstance.
The truths you have told, and the purity of the
language in which they are expressed, as your *Journey*
is universally read, may, and already appear to have
a very good effect. For a man of my acquaintance, who
has the largest nursery for trees and hedges in this
country, tells me, that of late the demand upon him
for these articles is doubled, and sometimes tripled.
I have, therefore, listed Dr. Samuel Johnson in some
of my memorandums of the principal planters and
favourers of the enclosures, under a name which I took
the liberty to invent from the Greek, *Papadendrion.*
Lord Auchinleck and some few more are of the list.
I am told that one gentleman in the shire of Aberdeen,
viz. Sir Archibald Grant, has planted above fifty
millions of trees on a piece of very wild ground at
Monimusk : I must enquire if he has fenced them well,
before he enters my list ; for, that is the soul of en-
closing.   I began myself to plant a little, our ground
being too valuable for much, and that is now fifty
years ago ; and the trees, now in my seventy-fourth
year, I look up to with reverence, and shew them to my

eldest son now in his fifteenth year, and they are full
the heighth of my country-house here, where I had the
pleasure of receiving you, and hope again to have
that satisfaction with our mutual friend, Mr. Boswell.
I shall always continue, with the truest esteem, dear
Doctor, your much obliged, and obedient humble
servant,

'ALEXANDER DICK.'

124. *Johnson to Boswell.* [1777].

'DEAR SIR,—I have been much pleased with your
late letter, and am glad that my old enemy, Mrs.
Boswell, begins to feel some remorse. As to Miss
Veronica's Scotch, I think it cannot be helped. An
English maid you might easily have; but she would
still imitate the greater number, as they would be likewise those whom she must most respect. Her dialect
will not be gross. Her Mamma has not much Scotch,
and you have yourself very little. I hope she knows
my name, and does not call me *Johnston*[1].

The immediate cause of my writing is this:—One
Shaw, who seems a modest and a decent man, has
written an *Erse Grammar*, which a very learned
Highlander, Macbean, has, at my request, examined
and approved.

'The book is very little, but Mr. Shaw has been
persuaded by his friends to set it at half a guinea,
though I advised only a crown, and thought myself liberal. You, whom the authour considers as a

---

[1] John*son* is the most common English formation of the
Sirname from *John*; John*ston* the Scotch. My illustrious friend
observed, that many North Britons pronounced his name in their
own way.

great encourager of ingenious men, will receive a parcel of his proposals and receipts. I have undertaken to give you notice of them, and to solicit your countenance. You must ask no poor man, because the price is really too high. Yet such a work deserves patronage.

'It is proposed to augment our club from twenty to thirty, of which I am glad; for as we have several in it whom I do not much like to consort with[1], I am for reducing it to a mere miscellaneous collection of conspicuous men, without any determinate character. ... I am, dear Sir, most affectionately your's,

'March 11, 1777.'   'SAM. JOHNSON.'

125. *The Lives of the Poets* [1777].

'TO JAMES BOSWELL, ESQ.

'DEAR SIR,   'Southill, Sept. 26, 1777.

'You will find by this letter, that I am still in the same calm retreat, from the noise and bustle of London, as when I wrote to you last. I am happy to find you had such an agreeable meeting with your old friend Dr. Johnson; I have no doubt your stock is much increased by the interview; few men, nay I may say, scarcely any man, has got that fund of knowledge and entertainment as Dr. Johnson in conversation. When he opens freely, every one is attentive to what he says, and cannot fail of improvement as well as pleasure.

'The edition of the Poets, now printing, will do honour to the English press; and a concise account of

---

[1] On account of their differing from him as to religion and politicks.

he drawing by GEORGE DANCE in the National Portrait Gallery

e drawing by GEORGE DANCE in the National Portrait Gallery

with the proposal. As to the terms, it was left entirely to the Doctor to name his own: he mentioned two hundred guineas [1] : it was immediately agreed to; and a farther compliment, I believe, will be made him. A committee was likewise appointed to engage the best engravers, *viz.*, Bartolozzi, Sherwin, Hall, etc. Likewise another committee for giving directions about the paper, printing, &c., so that the whole will be conducted with spirit, and in the best manner, with respect to authourship, editorship, engravings, &c., &c. My brother will give you a list of the Poets we mean to give, many of which are within the time of the Act or Queen Anne, which Martin and Bell cannot give, as they have no property in them; the proprietors are almost all the booksellers in London, of consequence. I am, dear Sir, ever your's,

'EDWARD DILLY.'

126. *Irish Antiquities* [1777].

'DR. JOHNSON TO CHARLES O'CONNOR, ESQ.

'SIR,—Having had the pleasure of conversing with Dr. Campbell about your character and your literary undertaking, I am resolved to gratify myself by renewing a correspondence which began and ended a great while ago, and ended, I am afraid, by my fault; a

---

[1] Johnson's moderation in demanding so small a sum is extraordinary. Had he asked one thousand, or even fifteen hundred guineas, the booksellers, who knew the value of his name, would doubtless have readily given it. They have probably got five thousand guineas by this work in the course of twenty-five years. [M.]

fault which, if you have not forgotten it, you must now forgive.

'If I have ever disappointed you, give me leave to tell you, that you have likewise disappointed me. I expected great discoveries in Irish antiquity, and large publications in the Irish language; but the world still remains as it was, doubtful and ignorant. What the Irish language is in itself, and to what languages it has affinity, are very interesting questions, which every man wishes to see resolved that has any philological or historical curiosity. Dr. Leland begins his history too late: the ages which deserve an exact enquiry are those times (for such there were) when Ireland was the school of the west, the quiet habitation of sanctity and literature. If you could give a history, though imperfect, of the Irish nation, from its conversion to Christianity to the invasion from England, you would amplify knowledge with new views and new objects. Set about it therefore, if you can: do what you can easily do without anxious exactness. Lay the foundation, and leave the superstructure to posterity. I am Sir, your most humble servant,

'May 19, 1777.'   'SAM. JOHNSON.'

127. *Dedication to the King* [1777].

Early in this year came out, in two volumes quarto, the posthumous works of the learned Dr. Zachary Pearce, Bishop of Rochester; being *A Commentary, with Notes, on the four Evangelists and the Acts of the Apostles,* with other theological pieces. Johnson had now an opportunity of making a grateful return to

K 2

that excellent prelate, who, we have seen, was the only
person who gave him any assistance in the compilation
of his *Dictionary*.   The Bishop had left some account
of his life and character, written by himself.   To this
Johnson made some valuable additions, and also
furnished to the editor, the Reverend Mr. Derby, a
Dedication, which I shall here insert, both because
it will appear at this time with peculiar propriety; and
because it will tend to propagate and increase that
'fervour of *Loyalty*,' which in me, who boast of the
name of TORY, is not only a principle, but a passion.

'TO THE KING.

'SIR,—I presume to lay before your Majesty the
last labours of a learned Bishop, who died in the toils
and duties of his calling.   He is now beyond the reach
of all earthly honours and rewards; and only the hope
of inciting others to imitate him, makes it now fit to be
remembered, that he enjoyed in his life the favour of
your Majesty.

'The tumultuary life of Princes seldom permits
them to survey the wide extent of national interest,
without losing sight of private merit; to exhibit
qualities which may be imitated by the highest and the
humblest of mankind; and to be at once amiable and
great.

'Such characters, if now and then they appear in
history, are contemplated with admiration.   May it be
the ambition of all your subjects to make haste with
their tribute of reverence; and as posterity may learn
from your Majesty how Kings should live, may they

learn, likewise, from your people, how they should
be honoured.   I am, may it please your Majesty, with
the most profound respect, your Majesty's most duti-
ful and devoted   'Subject and Servant.'

128. *Johnson to Boswell* [1777].

'Sir Alexander Dick is the only Scotsman liberal
enough not to be angry that I could not find trees,
where trees were not.   I was much delighted by his
kind letter. . . . .

'I have dined lately with poor dear ———.   I do
not think he goes on well.   His table is rather coarse,
and he has his children too much about him.   But he
is a very good man.'

129. *Driving in a Post-chaise* [1777].

In our way, Johnson strongly expressed his love of
driving fast in a post-chaise.   'If (said he,) I had no
duties, and no reference to futurity, I would spend
my life in driving briskly in a post-chaise with a pretty
woman ; but she should be one who could understand
me, and would add something to the conversation.'

130. *Early Rising* [1777].

I talked of the difficulty of rising in the morning.
Dr. Johnson told me, ' that the learned Mrs. Carter, at
that period when she was eager in study, did not
awake as early as she wished, and she therefore had
a contrivance, that, at a certain hour, her chamber-
light should burn a string to which a heavy weight
was suspended, which then fell with a strong sudden
noise: this roused her from sleep, and then she had

no difficulty in getting up.' But I said *that* was my difficulty; and wished there could be some medicine invented which would make one rise without pain, which I never did, unless after lying in bed a very long time. Perhaps there may be something in the stores of Nature which could do this.

131. *Criticisms of Johnson's Style* [1777].

I mentioned to him that Dr. Hugh Blair, in his lectures on Rhetorick and Belles Lettres, which I heard him deliver at Edinburgh, had animadverted on the Johnsonian style as too pompous; and attempted to imitate it, by giving a sentence of Addison in *The Spectator*, No. 411, in the manner of Johnson. When treating of the utility of the pleasures of imagination in preserving us from vice, it is observed of those 'who know not how to be idle and innocent,' that 'their very first step out of business is into vice or folly;' which Dr. Blair supposed would have been expressed in *The Rambler*, thus: 'Their very first step out of the regions of business is into the perturbation of vice, or the vacuity of folly.' JOHNSON. 'Sir, these are not the words I should have used. No, Sir; the imitators of my style have not hit it. Miss Aikin has done it the best; for she has imitated the sentiment as well as the diction.' . . . .

I read to him a letter which Lord Monboddo had written to me, containing some critical remarks upon the style of his *Journey to the Western Islands of Scotland*. His Lordship praised the very fine passage upon landing at Icolmkill[1]; but his own style being exceedingly dry and hard, he disapproved of the richness of Johnson's language, and of his frequent use of metaphorical expressions. JOHNSON. 'Why, Sir, this criticism would be just, if in my style, superfluous words, or words too big for the thoughts, could be pointed out; but this I do not believe can be done. For instance; in the passage which Lord Monboddo admires,'We were now treading that illustrious region,' the word *illustrious*, contributes nothing to the mere narration; for the fact might be told without it: but it is not, therefore, superfluous; for it wakes the mind to peculiar attention, where something of more than usual importance is to be presented. " Illustrious !"—for what? and then the sentence proceeds to expand the circumstances connected with Iona. And, Sir, as to metaphorical expression, that is a

---

[1] 'We were now treading that illustrious island, which was once the luminary of the Caledonian regions, whence savage clans and roving barbarians derived the benefits of knowledge, and the blessings of religion. To abstract the mind from all local emotion would be impossible, if it were endeavoured, and would be foolish, if it were possible. Whatever withdraws us from the power of our senses, whatever makes the past, the distant, or the future, predominate over the present, advances us in the dignity of thinking beings. Far from me, and from my friends, be such frigid philosophy, as may conduct us, indifferent and unmoved, over any ground which has been dignified by wisdom, bravery, or virtue. The man is little to be envied, whose patriotism would not gain force upon the plain of Marathon, or whose piety would not grow warmer among the ruins of Iona.'

Had our Tour produced nothing else but this sublime passage, the world must have acknowledged that it was not made in vain. Sir Joseph Banks, the present respectable President of the Royal Society, told me, he was so much struck on reading it, that he clasped his hands together, and remained for some time in an attitude of silent admiration.

great excellence in style, when it is used with propriety, for it gives you two ideas for one;—conveys the meaning more luminously, and generally with a perception of delight.'

132. *Tired of Life* [1777].

I suggested a doubt, that if I were to reside in London, the exquisite zest with which I relished it in occasional visits might go off, and I might grow tired of it. JOHNSON. 'Why, Sir, you find no man, at all intellectual, who is willing to leave London. No, Sir, when a man is tired of London, he is tired of life; for there is in London all that life can afford.'

133. *Colloquial Barbarisms* [1777].

He found fault with me for using the phrase to *make* money. 'Don't you see (said he,) the impropriety of it? To *make* money is to *coin* it: you should say *get* money.' The phrase, however, is, I think, pretty current. But Johnson was at all times jealous of infractions upon the genuine English language, and prompt to repress colloquial barbarisms; such as, *pledging myself,* for *undertaking; line,* for *department,* or *branch,* as the *civil line,* the *banking line.* He was particularly indignant against the almost universal use of the word *idea* in the sense of *notion* or *opinion,* when it is clear that *idea* can only signify something of which an image can be formed in the mind. We may have an *idea* or *image* of a mountain, a tree, a building: but we cannot surely have an *idea* or *image* of an *argument* or *proposition.* Yet we hear the sages of the law 'delivering their *ideas* upon the question under consideration;' and the first speakers in parliament 'entirely coinciding in the *idea* which has been ably stated by an honourable member;'—or 'reprobating an *idea* unconstitutional, and fraught with the most dangerous consequences to a great and free country.' Johnson called this 'modern cant.'

134. *The Slave Trade* [1777].

After supper I accompanied him to his apartment, and at my request he dictated to me an argument in favour of the negro who was then claiming his liberty, in an action in the Court of Session in Scotland. He had always been very zealous against slavery in every form, in which I with all deference thought that he discovered 'a zeal without knowledge.' . . . .

The argument dictated by Dr. Johnson, was as follows :—

'It must be agreed that in most ages many countries have had part of their inhabitants in a state of slavery; yet it may be doubted whether slavery can ever be supposed the natural condition of man. It is impossible not to conceive that men in their original state were equal; and very difficult to imagine how one would be subjected to another but by violent compulsion. An individual may, indeed, forfeit his liberty by a crime; but he cannot by that crime forfeit the liberty of his children. What is true of a criminal seems true likewise of a captive. A man may accept life from a conquering enemy on condition of perpetual servitude; but it is very doubtful whether he can entail that servitude on his descendants; for no man can stipulate without commission for another. The condition which he himself accepts, his son or grandson perhaps would have rejected. If we should admit, what perhaps may with more reason be denied, that there are certain relations between man and man which may make slavery necessary and just, yet it can never be proved that he who is now suing for his freedom ever stood in any of those relations. He is certainly subject by no law, but that of violence, to his present master; who pretends no claim to his obedience, but that he bought him from a merchant of slaves, whose right to sell him never was examined. It is said that according to the constitutions of Jamaica he was legally enslaved; these constitutions are merely positive; and apparently injurious to the rights of mankind, because whoever is exposed to sale is condemned to slavery without appeal; by whatever fraud or violence he might have been originally brought into the merchant's power. In our own time Princes have been sold, by wretches to whose care they were entrusted, that they might have an European education; but when once they were brought to a market in the plantations, little would avail either their dignity or their wrongs. The laws of Jamaica afford a Negro no redress. His colour is considered as a sufficient testimony against him. It is to be lamented that moral right should ever give way to political convenience. But if temptations of interest are sometimes too strong for human virtue, let us at least retain a virtue where there is no

temptation to quit it. In the present case there is
apparent right on one side, and no convenience on the
other. Inhabitants of this island can neither gain
riches nor power by taking away the liberty of any
part of the human species. The sum of the argument
is this:—No man is by nature the property of another :
The defendant is, therefore, by nature free : The
rights of nature must be some way forfeited before
they can be justly taken away : That the defendant
has by any act forfeited the rights of nature we
require to be proved ; and if no proof of such for-
feiture can be given, we doubt not but the justice
of the court will declare him free.'

135. *Hurd's Cowley* [1778].

He said, 'I was angry with Hurd about Cowley,
for having published a selection of his works : but,
upon better consideration, I think there is no impropriety in a man's publishing as much as he chooses of
any authour, if he does not put the rest out of the way.
A man, for instance, may print the *Odes* of Horace
alone.' He seemed to be in a more indulgent humour
than when this subject was discussed between him and
Mr. Murphy.

136. *Human Powers* [1778].

On Friday, April 3, I dined with him in London,
in a company where were present several eminent
men, whom I shall not name, but distinguish their parts
in the conversation by different letters.

F. 'I have been looking at this famous antique
marble dog of Mr. Jennings, valued at a thousand

guineas, said to be Alcibiades's dog.' JOHNSON.
'His tail then must be docked. That was the mark
of Alcibiades's dog.' E. 'A thousand guineas! The
representation of no animal whatever is worth so much.
At this rate a dead dog would indeed be better than a
living lion.' JOHNSON. 'Sir, it is not the worth of
the thing, but of the skill in forming it which is so.
highly estimated. Every thing that enlarges the
sphere of human powers, that shows man he can
do what he thought he could not do, is valuable.
The first man who balanced a straw upon his nose ;
Johnson, who rode upon three horses at a time ; in
short, all such men deserved the applause of mankind,
not on account of the use of what they did, but of the
dexterity which they exhibited.' BOSWELL. 'Yet
a misapplication of time and assiduity is not to be
encouraged. Addison, in one of his *Spectators*,
commends the judgement of a King, who as a suitable
reward to a man that by long perseverance had
attained to the art of throwing a barley-corn through
the eye of a needle, gave him a bushel of barley.'
JOHNSON. 'He must have been a King of Scotland,
where barley is scarce.' F. 'One of the most
remarkable antique figures of an animal is the boar at
Florence.' JOHNSON. 'The first boar that is well
made in marble, should be preserved as a wonder.
When men arrive at a facility of making boars well,
then the workmanship is not of such value, but they
should however be preserved as examples, and as a
greater security for the restoration of the art, should
it be lost.'

137. *Virtues and Vices* [1778].

E. 'From the experience which I have had,—and I have had a great deal,—I have learnt to think *better* of mankind.' JOHNSON. 'From my experience I have found them worse in commercial dealings, more disposed to cheat, than I had any notion of; but more disposed to do one another good than I had conceived.' J. 'Less just and more beneficent.' JOHNSON. 'And really it is wonderful, considering how much attention is necessary for men to take care of themselves, and ward off immediate evils which press upon them, it is wonderful how much they do for others. As it is said of the greatest liar, that he tells more truth than falsehood; so it may be said of the worst man, that he does more good than evil.' BOSWELL. 'Perhaps from experience men may be found *happier* than we suppose.' JOHNSON. 'No, Sir; the more we enquire, we shall find men the less happy.'

138. *Diffusion of Good Writing* [1778].

He asked me to go down with him and dine at Mr. Thrale's at Streatham, to which I agreed. I had lent him *An Account of Scotland, in 1702*, written by a man of various enquiry, an English chaplain to a regiment stationed there. JOHNSON. 'It is sad stuff, Sir, miserably written, as books in general then were. There is now an elegance of style universally diffused. No man now writes so ill as Martin's *Account of the Hebrides* is written. A man could

not write so ill, if he should ’try. Set a merchant’s
clerk now to write, and he’ll do better.’ . . . .
‘All the latter preachers have a good style. Indeed,
nobody now talks much of style; every body com-
poses pretty well. There are no such inharmonious
periods as there were a hundred years ago.’

139. *London and Minorca* [1778].

I mentioned to him that I had become very weary
in a company where I heard not a single intellectual
sentence, except that ‘a man who had been settled
ten years in Minorca was become a much inferiour
man to what he was in London, because a man’s mind
grows narrow in a narrow place.’ JOHNSON. ‘A
man’s mind grows narrow in a narrow place, whose
mind is enlarged only because he has lived in a large
place; but what is got by books and thinking is
preserved in a narrow place as well as in a large
place. A man cannot know modes of life as well
in Minorca as in London; but he may study mathematicks as well in Minorca.’ BOSWELL. ‘I don’t
know, Sir: if you had remained ten years in the Isle
of Col, you would not have been the man that
you now are.’ JOHNSON. ‘Yes, Sir, if I had been
there from fifteen to twenty-five; but not if from
twenty-five to thirty-five.’ BOSWELL. ‘I own, Sir,
the spirits which I have in London make me do
every thing with more readiness and vigour. I can
talk twice as much in London as any where else.’

140. *Scotland* [1778].

At dinner, Mrs. Thrale expressed a wish to go and see Scotland. JOHNSON. 'Seeing Scotland, Madam, is only seeing a worse England. It is seeing the flower gradually fade away to the naked stalk. Seeing the Hebrides, indeed, is seeing quite a different scene.'

141. *A Soldier's Grievance* [1778].

The Bishop said, it appeared from Horace's writings that he was a cheerful contented man. JOHNSON. 'We have no reason to believe that, my Lord. Are we to think Pope was happy, because he says so in his writings? We see in his writings what he wished the state of his mind to appear. Dr. Young, who pined for preferment, talks with contempt of it in his writings, and affects to despise every thing that he did not despise.' BISHOP OF ST. ASAPH. 'He was like other chaplains, looking for vacancies: but that is not peculiar to the clergy. I remember when I was with the army, after the battle of Lafeldt, the officers seriously grumbled that no general was killed.'

142. *Tardiness of Locomotion* [1778].

Goldsmith being mentioned, Johnson observed, that it was long before his merit came to be acknowledged. That he once complained to him, in ludicrous terms of distress, 'Whenever I write any thing, the publick *make a point* to know nothing about it:' but that his *Traveller* brought him into high reputation. LANGTON. 'There is not one bad line in that poem;

not one of Dryden's careless verses.' SIR JOSHUA. 'I was glad to hear Charles Fox say, it was one of the finest poems in the English language.' LANGTON. 'Why was you glad? You surely had no doubt of this before.' JOHNSON. 'No; the merit of *The Traveller* is so well established, that Mr. Fox's praise cannot augment it, nor his censure diminish it.' SIR JOSHUA. 'But his friends may suspect they had too great a partiality for him.' JOHNSON. 'Nay, Sir, the partiality of his friends was always against him. It was with difficulty we could give him a hearing. Goldsmith had no settled notions upon any subject; so he talked always at random. It seemed to be his intention to blurt out whatever was in his mind, and see what would become of it. He was angry too, when catched in an absurdity; but it did not prevent him from falling into another the next minute. I remember Chamier, after talking with him for some time, said, " Well, I do believe he wrote this poem him-self: and, let me tell you, that is believing a great deal." Chamier once asked him, what he meant by *slow*, the last word in the first line of *The Traveller*,

"Remote, unfriended, melancholy, slow."

Did he mean tardiness of locomotion? Goldsmith, who would say something without consideration, answered, "Yes." I was sitting by, and said, "No, Sir; you do not mean tardiness of locomotion; you mean, that sluggishness of mind which comes upon a man in solitude." Chamier believed then that I had written the line as much as if he had seen me write it. Goldsmith, however, was a man, who, whatever he wrote, did it better than any other man could do. He deserved a place in Westminster-Abbey, and every year he lived, would have deserved it better. He had, indeed, been at no pains to fill his mind with know-ledge. He transplanted it from one place to another; and it did not settle in his mind; so he could not tell what was in his own books.'

143. *Old Age* [1778].

We talked of old age. Johnson (now in his seven-tieth year,) said, ' It is a man's own fault, it is from want of use, if his mind grows torpid in old age.' The Bishop asked, if an old man does not lose faster than he gets. JOHNSON. 'I think not, my Lord, if he exerts himself.' One of the company rashly observed, that he thought it was happy for an old man that insensibility comes upon him. JOHNSON. (with a noble elevation and disdain,) ' No, Sir, I should never be happy by being less rational.' BISHOP OF ST. ASAPH. ' Your wish then, Sir, is γηράσκειν διδασκόμενος.' JOHNSON. 'Yes, my Lord.'

144. *Numerous Prose* [1778].

When we went to the drawing-room there was a rich assemblage. Besides the company who had been at dinner, there were Mr. Garrick, Mr. Harris of Salisbury, Dr. Percy, Dr. Burney, Honourable Mrs. Cholmondeley, Miss Hannah More, &c. &c.

After wandering about in a kind of pleasing distraction for some time, I got into a corner, with Johnson, Garrick, and Harris. GARRICK: (to Harris.)

'Pray, Sir, have you read Potter's *Æschylus*?'
HARRIS. 'Yes; and think it pretty.' GARRICK. (to
Johnson.) 'And what think you, Sir, of it?' JOHNSON.
'I thought what I read of it *verbiage*: but upon Mr.
Harris's recommendation, I will read a play. (To Mr.
Harris.) Don't prescribe two.' Mr. Harris suggested
one, I do not remember which. JOHNSON. 'We must
try its effect as an English poem; that is the way
to judge of the merit of a translation. Translations
are, in general, for people who cannot read the
original.' I mentioned the vulgar saying, that Pope's
Homer was not a good representation of the original.
JOHNSON. 'Sir, it is the greatest work of the kind
that has ever been produced.' BOSWELL. 'The
truth is, it is impossible perfectly to translate poetry.
In a different language it may be the same tune, but it
has not the same tone. Homer plays it on a bassoon;
Pope on a flagelet.' HARRIS. 'I think Heroick poetry
is best in blank verse; yet it appears that rhyme
is essential to English poetry, from our deficiency in
metrical quantities. In my opinion, the chief excellence of our language is numerous prose.' JOHNSON.
'Sir William Temple was the first writer who gave
cadence to English prose. Before his time they were
careless of arrangement, and did not mind whether a
sentence ended with an important word or an
insignificant word, or with what part of speech it was
concluded.' Mr. Langton, who now had joined us,
commended Clarendon. JOHNSON. 'He is objected
to for his parentheses, his involved clauses, and his
want of harmony. But he is supported by his matter.

It is, indeed, owing to a plethory of matter that his style is so faulty. Every *substance* (smiling to Mr. Harris,) has so many *accidents*.—To be distinct, we must talk *analytically*. If we analyse language, we must speak of it grammatically; if we analyse argument, we must speak of it logically.'

145. *Soldiers and Sailors* [1778].

We talked of war. JOHNSON. 'Every man thinks meanly of himself for not having been a soldier, or not having been at sea.' BOSWELL. 'Lord Mansfield does not.' JOHNSON. 'Sir, if Lord Mansfield were in a company of General Officers and Admirals who have been in service, he would shrink; he'd wish to creep under the table.' BOSWELL. 'No; he'd think he could *try* them all.' JOHNSON. 'Yes, if he could catch them: but they'd try him much sooner. No, Sir; were Socrates and Charles the Twelfth of Sweden both present in any company, and Socrates to say, "Follow me, and hear a lecture in philosophy;" and Charles, laying his hand on his sword, to say, "Follow me, and dethrone the Czar;" a man would be ashamed to follow Socrates. Sir, the impression is universal; yet it is strange. As to the sailor, when you look down from the quarter deck to the space below, you see the utmost extremity of human misery; such crouding, such filth, such stench!' BOSWELL. 'Yet sailors are happy.' JOHNSON. 'They are happy as brutes are happy, with a piece of fresh meat,—with the grossest sensuality. But, Sir, the profession of soldiers and sailors has the dignity of danger. Mankind reverence those who have got over fear, which is so general a weakness.' SCOTT. 'But is not courage mechanical, and to be acquired?' JOHNSON. 'Why yes, Sir, in a collective sense. Soldiers consider themselves only as parts of a great machine.' SCOTT. 'We find people fond of being sailors.' JOHNSON. 'I cannot account for that, any more than I can account for other strange perversions of imagination.'

His abhorrence of the profession of a sailor was uniformly violent; but in conversation he always exalted the profession of a soldier. And yet I have, in my large and various collection of his writings, a letter to an eminent friend, in which he expresses himself thus: ' My god-son called on me lately. He is weary, and rationally weary, of a military life. If you can place him in some other state, I think you may increase his happiness, and secure his virtue. A soldier's time is passed in distress and danger, or in idleness and corruption.' Such was his cool reflection in his study; but whenever he was warmed and animated by the presence of company, he, like other philosophers, whose minds are impregnated with poetical fancy, caught the common enthusiasm for splendid renown.

146. *The Wall of China* [1778].

He talked with an uncommon animation of travelling into distant countries; that the mind was enlarged by it, and that an acquisition of dignity of character was derived from it. He expressed a particular enthusiasm with respect to visiting the wall of China. I catched it for the moment, and said I really believed

I should go and see the wall of China had I not
children, of whom it was my duty to take care.
' Sir, (said he,) by doing so, you would do what would
be of importance in raising your children to eminence.
There would be a lustre reflected upon them from
your spirit and curiosity. They would be at all times
regarded as the children of a man who had gone to
view the wall of China. I am serious, Sir.'

147. *Ravenous Reading* [1778].

At Mr. Dilly's to-day were Mrs. Knowles, the
ingenious Quaker lady, Miss Seward, the poetess of
Lichfield, the Reverend Dr. Mayo, and the Rev.
Mr. Beresford, Tutor to the Duke of Bedford. Before
dinner Dr. Johnson seized upon Mr. Charles Sheridan's
Account of the late Revolution in Sweden, and seemed
to read it ravenously, as if he devoured it, which was
to all appearance his method of studying. 'He knows
how to read better than any one (said Mrs. Knowles;)
he gets at the substance of a book directly; he tears
out the heart of it.' He kept it wrapt up in the
tablecloth in his lap during the time of dinner, from an
avidity to have one entertainment in readiness when
he should have finished another; resembling (if I may
use so coarse a simile) a dog who holds a bone in his
paws in reserve, while he eats something else which
has been thrown to him.

148. *Flattery* [1778].

Talking of Miss——, a literary lady, he said,
' I was obliged to speak to Miss Reynolds, to let her

know that I desired she would not flatter me so much.'
Somebody now observed, 'She flatters Garrick.'
JOHNSON. 'She is in the right to flatter Garrick.
She is in the right for two reasons; first, because she
has the world with her, who have been praising
Garrick these thirty years; and secondly, because she
is rewarded for it by Garrick. Why should she
flatter *me*? I can do nothing for her. Let her carry
her praise to a better market. (Then turning to Mrs.
Knowles.) You, Madam, have been flattering me all the
evening; I wish you would give Boswell a little now.
If you knew his merit as well as I do, you would say
a great deal; he is the best travelling companion
in the world.'

149. *Travels* [1778].

I expressed some inclination to publish an account
of my *Travels* upon the continent of Europe, for
which I had a variety of materials collected. JOHNSON.
'I do not say, Sir, you may not publish your travels;
but I give you my opinion, that you would lessen
yourself by it. What can you tell of countries so well
known as those upon the continent of Europe, which
you have visited?' BOSWELL. 'But I can give an
entertaining narrative, with many incidents, anecdotes,
jeux d'esprit, and remarks, so as to make very pleasant
reading.' JOHNSON. 'Why, Sir, most modern travellers
in Europe who have published their travels, have
been laughed at: I would not have you added to the
number [1]. The world is now not contented to be

---

[1] I believe, however, I shall follow my own opinion; for the

merely entertained by a traveller's narrative; they want to learn something. Now some of my friends asked me, why I did not give some account of my travels in France. The reascn is plain; intelligent readers had seen more of France than I had. *You* might have liked my travels in France, and THE CLUB might have liked them; but, upon the whole, there would have been more ridicule than good produced by them.' BOSWELL. 'I cannot agree with you, Sir. People would like to read what you say of any thing. Suppose a face has been painted by fifty painters before; still we love to see it done by Sir Joshua.' JOHNSON. 'True, Sir, but Sir Joshua cannot paint a face when he has not time to look on it.' BOSWELL. 'Sir, a sketch of any sort by him is valuable. And, Sir, to talk to you in your own style (raising my voice, and shaking my head,) you *should* have given us your travels in France. I am *sure* I am right, and *there's an end on't*.'

I said to him that it was certainly true, as my friend Dempster had observed in his letter to me upon the subject, that a great part of what was in his *Journey to the Western Islands of Scotland* had been in his mind before he left London. JOHNSON. 'Why yes, Sir, the topicks were; and books of travels will be good in proportion to what a man has previously in his mind; his knowing what to observe; his power of contrasting one mode of life with another. As the Spanish proverb says, " He, who would bring home the wealth of the Indies, must carry the wealth of the

world has shewn a very flattering partiality to my writings, on many occasions.

Indies with him." So it is in travelling; a man must carry knowledge with him, if he would bring home knowledge.' BOSWELL. 'The proverb, I suppose, Sir, means, he must carry a large stock with him to trade with.' JOHNSON. 'Yes, Sir.'

150. *Johnson and Edwards* [1778].

EDWARDS. 'How do you live, Sir? For my part, I must have my regular meals, and a glass of good wine. I find I require it.' JOHNSON. 'I now drink no wine, Sir. Early in life I drank wine: for many years I drank none. I then for some years drank a great deal.' EDWARDS. 'Some hogsheads, I warrant you.' JOHNSON. 'I then had a severe illness, and left it off, and I have never begun it again. I never felt any difference upon myself from eating one thing rather than another, nor from one kind of weather rather than another. There are people, I believe, who feel a difference; but I am not one of them. And as to regular meals, I have fasted from the Sunday's dinner to the Tuesday's dinner, without any inconvenience. I believe it is best to eat just as one is hungry: but a man who is in business, or a man who has a family, must have stated meals. I am a straggler. I may leave this town and go to Grand Cairo, without being missed here or observed there.' EDWARDS. 'Don't you eat supper, Sir?' JOHNSON. 'No, Sir.' EDWARDS. 'For my part, now, I consider supper as a turnpike through which one must pass, in order to get to bed [1].'

---

[1] I am not absolutely sure but this was my own suggestion, though it is truly in the character of Edwards.

151. *Boswell is Tossed* [1778].

The Gentleman who had dined with us at Dr. Percy's came in. Johnson attacked the Americans with intemperate vehemence of abuse. I said something in their favour; and added, that I was always sorry when he talked on that subject. This, it seems, exasperated him; though he said nothing at the time. The cloud was charged with sulphureous vapour, which was afterwards to burst in thunder.—We talked of a gentleman who was running out his fortune in London; and I said, 'We must get him out of it. All his friends must quarrel with him, and that will soon drive him away.' JOHNSON. 'Nay, Sir, we'll send *you* to him. If your company does not drive a man out of his house, nothing will.' This was a horrible shock, for which there was no visible cause. I afterwards asked him why he had said so harsh a thing. JOHNSON. 'Because, Sir, you made me angry about the Americans.' BOSWELL. 'But why did you not take your revenge directly?' JOHNSON. (smiling) 'Because, Sir, I had nothing ready. A man cannot strike till he has his weapons.' This was a candid and pleasant confession.

152. *Wasting a Fortune* [1778].

On Monday, April 20, I found him at home in the morning. We talked of a gentleman who we apprehended was gradually involving his circumstances by bad management. JOHNSON. 'Wasting a fortune is evaporation by a thousand imperceptible means. If it were a stream, they'd stop it. You must speak to him. It is really miserable. Were he a gamester,

it could be said he had hopes of winning. Were he a
bankrupt in trade, he might have grown rich; but he
has neither spirit to spend nor resolution to spare.
He does not spend fast enough to have pleasure from
it. He has the crime of prodigality, and the wretchedness of parsimony. If a man is killed in a duel, he is
killed as many a one has been killed; but it is a sad
thing for a man to lie down and die; to bleed to death,
because he has not fortitude enough to sear the
wound, or even to stitch it up.' I cannot but pause a
moment to admire the fecundity of fancy, and choice
of language, which in this instance, and, indeed, on
almost all occasions, he displayed. It was well observed by Dr. Percy, now Bishop of Dromore, 'The
conversation of Johnson is strong and clear, and
may be compared to an antique statue, where every
vein and muscle is distinct and bold. Ordinary conversation resembles an inferiour cast.'

153. *Demosthenes Taylor* [1778].

He proceeded:—'Demosthenes Taylor, as he was
called, (that is, the Editor of Demosthenes) was the
most silent man, the merest statue of a man that I have
ever seen. I once dined in company with him, and all
he said during the whole time was no more than
Richard. How a man should say only Richard, it is
not easy to imagine. But it was thus: Dr. Douglas
was talking of Dr. Zachary Grey, and ascribing to him
something that was written by Dr. Richard Grey. So,
to correct him, Taylor said, (imitating his affected
sententious emphasis and nod,) " *Richard.*" '

154. *A Staffordshire Whig* [1778].

BOSWELL. 'I drank chocolate, Sir, this morning with Mr. Eld; and, to my no small surprize, found him to be a *Staffordshire Whig*, a being which I did not believe had existed.' JOHNSON. 'Sir, there are rascals in all countries.'

155. *Wine* [1778].

We talked of drinking wine. JOHNSON. 'I require wine, only when I am alone. I have then often wished for it, and often taken it.' SPOTTISWOODE. 'What, by way of a companion, Sir?' JOHNSON. 'To get rid of myself, to send myself away. Wine gives great pleasure; and every pleasure is of itself a good. It is a good, unless counterbalanced by evil. A man may have a strong reason not to drink wine; and that may be greater than the pleasure. Wine makes a man better pleased with himself. I do not say that it makes him more pleasing to others. Sometimes it does. But the danger is, that while a man grows better pleased with himself, he may be growing less pleasing to others. Wine gives a man nothing. It neither gives him knowledge nor wit; it only animates a man, and enables him to bring out what a dread of the company has repressed. It only puts in motion what has been locked up in frost. But this may be good, or it may be bad.' SPOTTISWOODE. 'So, Sir, wine is a key which opens a box; but this box may be either full or empty.' JOHNSON. 'Nay, Sir, conversation is the key: wine is a pick-lock, which forces open the box and injures it. A man should cultivate his mind so as to have that confidence and readiness without wine, which wine gives.'

156. *Johnson's Admirers* [1778].

On Wednesday, April 29, I dined with him at Mr. Allan Ramsay's, where were Lord Binning, Dr. Robertson the historian, Sir Joshua Reynolds, and the Honourable Mrs. Boscawen, widow of the Admiral, and mother of the present Viscount Falmouth; of whom, if it be not presumptuous in me to praise her, I would say, that her manners are the most agreeable, and her conversation the best, of any lady with whom I ever had the happiness to be acquainted. - Before Johnson came we talked a good deal of him; Ramsay said he had always found him a very polite man, and that he treated him with great respect, which he did very sincerely. I said I worshipped him. ROBERTSON. 'But some of you spoil him; you should not worship him; you should worship no man.' BOSWELL. 'I cannot help worshipping him, he is so much superior to other men.' ROBERTSON. 'In criticism, and in wit in conversation, he is no doubt very excellent; but in other respects he is not above other men; he will believe any thing, and will strenuously defend the most minute circumstance connected with the Church of England.' BOSWELL. 'Believe me, Doctor, you are much mistaken as to this; for when you talk with him calmly in private, he is very liberal in his way of thinking.' ROBERTSON. 'He and I have been always very gracious; the first time I met him was one evening at Strahan's, when he had just had an unlucky altercation with Adam Smith, to whom he had been so rough, that Strahan, after

Smith was gone, had remonstrated with him, and told him that I was coming soon, and that he was uneasy to think that he might behave in the same manner to me. "No, no, Sir, (said Johnson) I warrant you Robertson and I shall do very well." Accordingly he was gentle and good-humoured, and courteous with me the whole evening; and he has been so upon every occasion that we have met since. I have often said (laughing) that I have been in a great measure indebted to Smith for my good reception.' BOSWELL. 'His power of reasoning is very strong, and he has a peculiar art of drawing characters, which is as rare as good portrait painting.' SIR JOSHUA REYNOLDS. 'He is undoubtedly admirable in this; but, in order to mark the characters which he draws, he overcharges them, and gives people more than they really have, whether of good or bad.'

No sooner did he, of whom we had been thus talking so easily, arrive, than we were all as quiet as a school upon the entrance of the head-master; and were very soon set down to a table covered with such variety of good things, as contributed not a little to dispose him to be pleased.

157. *The King of Siam* [1778].

Johnson harangued against drinking wine. 'A man, (said he) may choose whether he will have abstemiousness and knowledge, or claret and ignorance.' Dr. Robertson, (who is very companionable,) was beginning to dissent as to the proscription of claret. JOHNSON: (with a placid smile.) 'Nay, Sir, you shall not differ with me; as I have said that the man is most perfect who takes in the most things, I am for knowledge and claret.' ROBERTSON: (holding a glass of generous claret in his hand.) 'Sir, I can only drink your health.' JOHNSON. 'Sir, I should be sorry if *you* should be ever in such a state as to be able to do nothing more.' ROBERTSON. 'Dr. Johnson, allow me to say, that in one respect I have the advantage of you; when you were in Scotland you would not come to hear any of our preachers, whereas, when I am here, I attend your publick worship without scruple, and indeed, with great satisfaction.' JOHNSON. 'Why, Sir, that is not so extraordinary: the King of Siam sent ambassadors to Louis the Fourteenth; but Louis the Fourteenth sent none to the King of Siam.'

158. *They talk of Runts* [1778].

JOHNSON. 'Mrs. Thrale's mother said of me what flattered me much. A clergyman was complaining of want of society in the country where he lived; and said, "They talk of *runts*;" (that is, young cows). "Sir, (said Mrs. Salusbury,) Mr. Johnson would learn to talk of runts:" meaning that I was a man who would make the most of my situation, whatever it was.' He added, 'I think myself a very polite man.'

159. *A Quarrel and Reconciliation* [1778].

On Saturday, May 2, I dined with him at Sir Joshua Reynolds's, where there was a very large company, and a great deal of conversation; but owing to some circumstance which I cannot now recollect, I have no record of any part of it, except that there were several people there by no means of the Johnsonian school; so that less attention was paid to him than usual, which put him out of humour; and upon some imaginary offence from me, he attacked me with such rudeness, that I was vexed and angry, because it gave those persons an opportunity of enlarging upon his supposed ferocity, and ill treatment of his best friends. I was so much hurt, and had my pride so much roused, that I kept away from him for a week; and, perhaps, might have kept away much longer, nay, gone to Scotland without seeing him again, had not we fortunately met and been reconciled. To such unhappy chances are human friendships liable.

On Friday, May 8, I dined with him at Mr. Langton's. I was reserved and silent, which I suppose he perceived, and might recollect the cause. After dinner, when Mr. Langton was called out of the room, and we were by ourselves, he drew his chair near to mine, and said, in a tone of conciliating courtesy, 'Well, how have you done?' BOSWELL. 'Sir, you have made me very uneasy by your behaviour to me when we were last at Sir Joshua Reynolds's. You know, my dear Sir, no man has a greater respect and affection for you, or would sooner go to the end of the world to serve you. Now to treat me so—.' He insisted that I had interrupted him, which I assured him was not the case; and proceeded—'But why treat me so before people who neither love you nor me?' JOHNSON. 'Well, I am sorry for it. I'll make it up to you twenty different ways, as you please.' BOSWELL.

'I said to-day to Sir Joshua, when he observed that you *tossed* me sometimes—I don't care how often, or how high he tosses me, when only friends are present, for then I fall upon soft ground: but I do not like falling on stones, which is the case when enemies are present.—I think this a pretty good image, Sir.' JOHNSON. 'Sir, it is one of the happiest I have ever heard.'

160. *A Man whom every body likes.*
[1778. *Johnson to Boswell*].

'You are now happy enough. Mrs. Boswell is recovered; and I congratulate you upon the probability of her long life. If general approbation will add anything to your enjoyment, I can tell you that I have heard you mentioned as *a man whom everybody likes.* I think life has little more to give.

[1779. *Boswell to Johnson*].

'They received me with the kindness of an old acquaintance; and after we had joined in a cordial chorus to *your* praise, Mrs. Cobb gave *me* the high satisfaction of hearing that you said "Boswell is a man who I believe never left a house without leaving a wish for his return."'

161. *London* [1779].

I was amused by considering with how much ease and coolness he could write or talk to a friend, exhorting him not to suppose that happiness was not to be found as well in other places as in London: when he himself was at all times sensible of its being, comparatively speaking, a heaven upon earth. The truth is, that by those who from sagacity, attention, and experience, have learnt the full advantage of London, its pre-eminence over every other place, not only for variety of enjoyment, but for comfort, will be felt with a philosophical exultation. The freedom from remark and petty censure, with which life may be passed there, is a circumstance which a man who knows the teazing restraint of a narrow circle must relish highly. Mr. Burke, whose orderly and amiable domestic habits might make the eye of observation less irksome to him than to most men, said once very pleasantly, in my hearing, 'Though I have the honour to represent Bristol, I should not like to live there; I should be obliged to be so much *upon my good behaviour.*' In London, a man may live in splendid society at one time, and in frugal retirement at another, without animadversion. There, and there alone, a man's own house is truly his *castle*, in which he can be in perfect safety from intrusion whenever he pleases. I never shall forget how well this was expressed to me one day by Mr. Meynell: 'The chief advantage of London (said he) is, that a man is always *so near his burrow.*'

162. *Read any Book* [1779].

'I am always for getting a boy forward in his learn-ing; for that is a sure good. I would let him at first read *any* English book which happens to engage his attention; because you have done a great deal when you have brought him to have entertainment from a book. He'll get better books afterwards.'

163. *Garrick* [1779].

On Saturday, April 24, I dined with him at Mr. Beauclerk's, with Sir Joshua Reynolds, Mr. Jones, (afterwards Sir William,) Mr. Langton, Mr. Steevens, Mr. Paradise, and Dr. Higgins. I mentioned that Mr. Wilkes had attacked Garrick to me, as a man who had no friend. ' I believe he is right, Sir. Οἱ φίλοι, οὐ φίλος—He had friends, but no friend. Garrick was so diffused, he had no man to whom he wished to unbosom himself. He found people always ready to applaud him, and that always for the same thing: so he saw life with great uniformity.' I took upon me, for once, to fight with Goliath's weapons, and play the sophist.—'Garrick did not need a friend, as he got from everybody all he wanted. What is a friend? One who supports you and comforts you, while others do not. Friendship, you know, Sir, is the cordial drop, " to make the nauseous draught of life go down :" but if the draught be not nauseous, if it be all sweet, there is no occasion for that drop.' JOHNSON. 'Many men would not be content to live so. I hope I should not. They would wish to have an intimate friend, with whom they might compare minds, and cherish private virtues.' One of the company mentioned Lord Chesterfield, as a man who had no friend. JOHNSON. 'There were more materials to make friendship in Garrick, had he not been so diffused.' BOSWELL. 'Garrick was pure gold, but beat out to thin leaf. Lord Chesterfield was tinsel.' JOHNSON. 'Garrick was a very good man, the cheerfullest man of his

age; a decent liver in a profession which is supposed
to give indulgence to licentiousness; and a man who
gave away, freely, money acquired by himself. . He
began the world with a great hunger for money; the
son of a half-pay officer, bred in a family, whose study
was to make four-pence do as much as others made
four-pence halfpenny do. But, when he had got
money, he was very liberal.' I presumed to animad-
vert on his eulogy on Garrick, in his *Lives of the
Poets*. 'You say, Sir, his death eclipsed the gaiety of
nations.' JOHNSON. 'I could not have said more
nor less. It is the truth; *eclipsed*, not *extinguished*;
and his death *did* eclipse; it was like a storm.'
BOSWELL. 'But why nations? Did his gaiety extend
farther than his own nation?' JOHNSON. 'Why, Sir,
some exaggeration must be allowed. Besides, nations
may be said—if we allow the Scotch to be a nation,
and to have gaiety,—which they have not. *You* are an
exception, though. Come, gentlemen, let us candidly
admit that there is one Scotchman who is cheerful.'
BEAUCLERK. 'But he is a very unnatural Scotchman.'

164. *Beauclerk* [1779].

Mr. Beauclerk was very entertaining this day, and
told us a number of short stories in a lively elegant
manner, and with that air of *the world* which has
I know not what impressive effect, as if there were
something more than is expressed, or than perhaps
we could perfectly understand. As Johnson and I
accompanied Sir Joshua Reynolds in his coach, Johnson
said, 'There is in Beauclerk a predominance over

his company, that one does not like. But he is a man who has lived so much in the world, that he has a short story on every occasion; he is always ready to talk, and is never exhausted.'

165. *Unemployment* [1779].

We talked of the state of the poor in London.— JOHNSON. 'Saunders Welch, the Justice, who was once High-Constable of Holborn, and had the best opportunities of knowing the state of the poor, told me, that I under-rated the number, when I computed that twenty a week, that is, above a thousand a year, died of hunger; not absolutely of immediate hunger; but of the wasting and other diseases which are the consequences of hunger. This happens only in so large a place as London, where people are not known. What we are told about the great sums got by begging is not true; the trade is overstocked. And, you may depend upon it, there are many who cannot get work. A particular kind of manufacture fails: Those who have been used to work at it, can, for some time, work at nothing else. You meet a man begging; you charge him with idleness: he says, "I am willing to labour. Will you give me work?"—"I cannot."— "Why then you have no right to charge me with idleness."'

166. *Union with Ireland* [1779].

He, I know not why, shewed upon all occasions an aversion to go to Ireland, where I proposed to him that we should make a tour. JOHNSON. 'It is the

last place where I should wish to travel.' BOSWELL.
'Should you not like to see Dublin, Sir?' JOHNSON.
'No, Sir! Dublin is only a worse capital.' BOSWELL.
'Is not the Giant's-Causeway worth seeing?' JOHNSON.
'Worth seeing? yes; but not worth going to see.'

Yet he had a kindness for the Irish nation, and thus generously expressed himself to a gentleman from that country, on the subject of an UNION which artful Politicians have often had in view—'Do not make an union with us, Sir. We should unite with you, only to rob you. We should have robbed the Scotch, if they had had any thing of which we could have robbed them.'

167. *Bereavement* [1780].

'TO DR. LAWRENCE.

'. . . . The loss, dear Sir, which you have lately suffered, I felt many years ago, and know therefore how much has been taken from you, and how little help can be had from consolation. He that outlives a wife whom he has long loved, sees himself disjoined from the only mind that has the same hopes, and fears, and interest; from the only companion with whom he has shared much good or evil; and with whom he could set his mind at liberty, to retrace the past or anticipate the future. The continuity of being is lacerated; the settled course of sentiment and action is stopped; and life stands suspended and motionless till it is driven by external causes into a new channel. But the time of suspense is dreadful.

'Our first recourse in this distressed solitude, is, perhaps for want of habitual piety, to a gloomy acquiescence in necessity. Of two mortal beings, one must lose the other; but surely there is a higher and better comfort to be drawn from the consideration of that Providence which watches over all, and a belief that the living and the dead are equally in the hands of GOD, who will reunite those whom he has separated; or who sees that it is best not to reunite. I am, dear Sir, your most affectionate, and most humble servant,

'January 20, 1780.'　　　　　　'SAM. JOHNSON.'

168. *Death of Beauclerk* [1780. *Letter to Boswell*].

'Poor dear Beauclerk—*nec, ut soles, dabis joca.* His wit and his folly, his acuteness and maliciousness, his merriment and reasoning, are now over. Such another will not often be found among mankind. He directed himself to be buried by the side of his mother, an instance of tenderness which I hardly expected. He has left his children to the care of Lady Di, and if she dies, of Mr. Langton, and of Mr. Leicester his relation, and a man of good character. His library has been offered to sale to the Russian ambassador[1].'

169. *Beauclerk's Wit* [1780].

From Mr. Langton I received soon after this time a letter, of which I extract a passage, relative both to Mr. Beauclerk and Dr. Johnson.

'The melancholy information you have received concerning Mr. Beauclerk's death is true. Had his

[1] Mr. Beauclerk's library was sold by publick auction in April and May 1781, for 5011 *l.* [M.]

talents been directed in any sufficient degree as they ought, I have always been strongly of opinion that they were calculated to make an illustrious figure; and that opinion, as it had been in part formed upon Dr. Johnson's judgment, receives more and more confirmation by hearing, what since his death, Dr. Johnson has said concerning them; a few evenings ago, he was at Mr. Vesey's, where Lord Althorpe, who was one of a numerous company there, addressed Dr. Johnson on the subject of Mr. Beauclerk's death, saying, "Our CLUB has had a great loss since we met last." He replied, "A loss, that perhaps the whole nation could not repair!" The Doctor then went on to speak of his endowments, and particularly extolled the wonderful ease with which he uttered what was highly excellent. He said, that "no man ever was so free when he was going to say a good thing, from a *look* that expressed that it was coming; or, when he had said it, from a look that expressed that it had come." At Mr. Thrale's, some days before when we were talking on the same subject, he said, referring to the same idea of his wonderful facility, "That Beauclerk's talents were those which he had felt himself more disposed to envy, than those of any whom he had known."'

170. *Idleness. Pope.* [1780. *Communicated by Langton*].

'He would allow no settled indulgence of idleness upon principle, and always repelled every attempt to urge excuses for it. A friend one day suggested, that it was not wholesome to study soon after dinner. JOHNSON. "Ah, Sir, don't give way to fancy. At one time of my life I had taken it into my head that it was not wholesome to study between breakfast and dinner."'

'Mr. Beauclerk one day repeated to Dr. Johnson, Pope's lines,

> "Let modest Foster, if he will, excel
> Ten metropolitans in preaching well:"

Then asked the Doctor, "Why did Pope say this?" JOHNSON. "Sir, he hoped it would vex somebody."'

171. *Queen Elizabeth* [1780. *Langton*].

'His distinction of the different degrees of attainment of learning was thus marked upon two occasions. Of Queen Elizabeth he said, "She had learning enough to have given dignity to a bishop;" and of Mr. Thomas Davies he said, "Sir, Davies has learning enough to give credit to a clergyman."'

172. *Burke* [1780. *Langton*].

'He used frequently to observe, that men might be very eminent in a profession, without our perceiving any particular power of mind in them in conversation. It seems strange (said he) that a man should see so far to the right, who sees so short a way to the left. Burke is the only man whose common conversation corresponds with the general fame which he has in the world. Take up whatever topick you please, he is ready to meet you."'

173. *Goldsmith* [1780. *Langton*].

'Of Dr. Goldsmith he said, "No man was more foolish when he had not a pen in hand, or more wise when he had."'

174. *The Lives of the Poets* [1781].

In 1781 Johnson at last completed his *Lives of the Poets*, of which he gives this account: 'Some time in March I finished the *Lives of the Poets*, which I wrote in my usual way, dilatorily and hastily, unwilling to work, and working with vigour and haste.' In a memorandum previous to this, he says of them: 'Written, I hope, in such a manner as may tend to the promotion of piety.'

This is the work which of all Dr. Johnson's writings will perhaps be read most generally, and with most pleasure. Philology and biography were his favourite pursuits, and those who lived most in intimacy with him, heard him upon all occasions, where there was a proper opportunity, take delight in expatiating upon the various merits of the English Poets: upon the niceties of their characters, and the events of their progress through the world which they contributed to illuminate. His mind was so full of that kind of information, and it was so well arranged in his memory, that in performing what he had undertaken in this way, he had little more to do than to put his thoughts upon paper, exhibiting first each Poet's life, and then subjoining a critical examination of his genius and works. But when he began to write, the

subject swelled in such a manner, that instead of prefaces to each poet, of no more than a few pages, as he
had originally intended, he produced an ample, rich,
and most entertaining view of them in every respect.

175. *The Life of Milton* [1781].

Against his Life of MILTON, the hounds of Whig-
gism have opened in full cry.   But of Milton's great
excellence as a poet, where shall we find such a
blazon as by the hand of Johnson?   I shall select only
the following passage concerning *Paradise Lost* :

' Fancy can hardly forbear to conjecture with what
temper Milton surveyed the silent progress of his
work, and marked his reputation stealing its way in a
kind of subterraneous current, through fear and silence.
I cannot but conceive him calm and confident, little
disappointed, not àt all dejected, relying on his own
merit with steady consciousness, and waiting without
impatience, the vicissitudes of opinion, and the im-
partiality of a future generation.' . . . .

That a man, who venerated the Church and Mon-
archy as Johnson did, should speak with a just abhorrence of Milton as a politician, or rather as a daring
foe to good polity, was surely to be expected; and
to those who censure him, I would recommend his
commentary on Milton's celebrated complaint of his
situation, when by the lenity of Charles the Second,
' a lenity of which (as Johnson well observes) the
world has had perhaps no other example, he, who
had written in justification of the murder of his Sovereign, was safe under an *Act of Oblivion.*'

' No sooner is he safe than he finds himself in danger, *fallen on evil days and evil tongues, with darkness and with danger compassed round.* This darkness, had his eyes been better employed, had undoubtedly deserved compassion; but to add the mention of danger, was ungrateful and unjust. He was fallen, indeed, on *evil days*; the time was come in which regicides could no longer boast their wickedness. But of *evil tongues* for Milton to complain, required impudence at least equal to his other powers; Milton, whose warmest advocates must allow, that he never spared any asperity of reproach, or brutality of insolence.'

176. *Imitations of Johnson* [1781].

Mr. Croft's performance was subjected to the revision of Dr. Johnson, as appears from the following note to Mr. John Nichols:

' This *Life of Dr. Young* was written by a friend of his son. What is crossed with black is expunged by the authour, what is crossed with red is expunged by me. If you find any thing more that can be well omitted, I shall not be sorry to see it yet shorter.'

It has always appeared to me to have a considerable share of merit, and to display a pretty successful imitation of Johnson's style. When I mentioned this to a very eminent literary character [1], he opposed me vehemently, exclaiming, ' No, no, it is *not* a good imitation of Johnson; it has all his pomp without his force; it has all the nodosities of the oak without its

---

[1] The late Mr. Burke. [M.]

strength.' This was an image so happy, that one might have thought he would have been satisfied with it; but he was not. And setting his mind again to work, he added, with exquisite felicity, 'It has all the contortions of the Sybil, without the inspiration.'

177. *Johnson to Warren Hastings* [1781].

'SIR,   'Jan. 9, 1781.

'Amidst the importance and multiplicity of affairs in which your great office engages you, I take the liberty of recalling your attention for a moment to literature, and will not prolong the interruption by an apology which your character makes needless.

'Mr. Hoole, a gentleman long known, and long esteemed in the India-House, after having translated Tasso, has undertaken Ariosto. How well he is qualified for his undertaking he has already shewn. He is desirous, Sir, of your favour in promoting his proposals, and flatters me by supposing that my testimony may advance his interest.

'It is a new thing for a clerk of the India-House to translate poets;—it is new for a Governour of Bengal to patronize learning. That he may find his ingenuity rewarded, and that learning may flourish under your protection, is the wish of, Sir, your most humble servant,

'SAM. JOHNSON.'

178. *Voracity* [1781].

Every thing about his character and manners was forcible and violent; there never was any moderation; many a day did he fast, many a year did he refrain from wine ; but when he did eat, it was voraciously ; when he did drink wine, it was copiously. He could practise abstinence, but not temperance.

179. *Quotation* [1781].

The subject of quotation being introduced, Mr. Wilkes censured it as pedantry. JOHNSON. 'No, Sir, it is a good thing; there is a community of mind in it. Classical quotation is the *parole* of literary men all over the world.' WILKES. 'Upon the continent they all quote the vulgate Bible. Shakspeare is chiefly quoted here; and we quote also Pope, Prior, Butler, Waller, and sometimes Cowley.'

180. *Bluestockings* [1781].

About this time it was much the fashion for several ladies to have evening assemblies, where the fair sex might participate in conversation with literary and ingenious men, animated by a desire to please. These societies were denominated *Blue-stocking Clubs*, the origin of which title being little known, it may be worth while to relate it. One of the most eminent members of those societies, when they first commenced, was Mr. Stillingfleet, whose dress was remarkably grave, and in particular it was observed, that he wore blue stockings. Such was the excellence of his conversation, that his absence was felt as so great a loss, that it used to be said, 'We can do nothing without the *blue-stockings*;' and thus by degrees the title was established. Miss Hannah More has admirably described a *Blue-stocking Club*, in her *Bas Bleu*, a poem in which many of the persons who were most conspicuous there are mentioned.

Johnson was prevailed with to come sometimes into these circles, and did not think himself too grave even for the lively Miss Monckton (now Countess of Corke) who used to have the finest *bit of blue* at the house of her mother, Lady Galway. Her vivacity enchanted the Sage, and they used to talk together with all imaginable ease. A singular instance happened one evening, when she insisted that some of Sterne's writings were very pathetick. Johnson bluntly denied it. 'I am sure (said she,) they have affected *me.*'— 'Why, (said Johnson, smiling, and rolling himself about,) that is, because, dearest, you're a dunce.' When she some time afterwards mentioned this to him, he said with equal truth and politeness; 'Madam, if I had thought so, I certainly should not have said it.'

181. *Publication by Subscription* [1781].

His disorderly habits, when 'making provision for the day that was passing over him,' appear from the following anecdote, communicated to me by Mr. John Nichols:—' In the year 1763, a young bookseller, who was an apprentice to Mr. Whiston, waited on him with a subscription to his *Shakspeare*: and observing that the Doctor made no entry in any book of the subscriber's name, ventured diffidently to ask, whether he would please to have the gentleman's address, that it might be properly inserted in the printed list of subscribers. '*I shall print no list of subscribers*;' said Johnson, with great abruptness: but almost immediately recollecting himself, added, very complacently, ' Sir, I have two very cogent reasons for not printing any list of subscribers;—one, that I have lost all the names,—the other, that I have spent all the money.'

182. *Of Tory and Whig* [1781].

One day, when I told him that I was a zealous Tory, but not enough ' according to knowledge,' and should be obliged to him for 'a reason,' he was so candid, and expressed himself so well, that I begged of him to repeat what he had said, and I wrote down as follows.

OF TORY AND WHIG.

' A wise Tory and a wise Whig, I believe, will agree. Their principles are the same, though their modes of thinking are different. A high Tory makes government unintelligible: it is lost in the clouds. A violent Whig makes it impracticable: he is for allowing so much liberty to every man, that there is not power enough to govern any man. The prejudice of the Tory is for establishment; the prejudice of the Whig is for innovation. A Tory does not wish to give more real power to Government; but that Government should have more reverence. Then they differ as to the Church. The Tory is not for giving more legal power to the Clergy, but wishes they should have a considerable influence, founded on the opinion of mankind; the Whig is for limiting and watching them with a narrow jealousy.'

183. *Letter to Chesterfield* [1781].

In the evening I put him in mind of his promise to favour me with a copy of his celebrated Letter to the Earl of Chesterfield, and he was at last pleased to comply with this earnest request, by dictating it to me from his memory ; for he believed that he himself had no copy. There was an animated glow in his countenance while he thus recalled his high-minded indignation.

184. *Chatterton* [1782].

To Edmond Malone, Esq.

'Dear Sir,—I hope I grow better, and shall soon be able to enjoy the kindness of my friends. I think this wild adherence to Chatterton [1] more unaccountable than the obstinate defence of Ossian. In Ossian there is a national pride, which may be forgiven, though it cannot be applauded. In Chatterton there is nothing but the resolution to say again what has once been said. I am, Sir, your humble servant,

'March 7, 1782.'   'Sam. Johnson.'

185. *Thrift* [1782. *Letters to Boswell*].

'Poverty, my dear friend, is so great an evil, and pregnant with so much temptation, and so much

---

[1] This note was in answer to one which accompanied one of the earliest pamphlets on the subject of Chatterton's forgery, entitled *Cursory Observations on the Poems attributed to Thomas Rowley*, &c. Mr. Thomas Warton's very able *Inquiry* appeared about three months afterwards ; and Mr. Tyrwhitt's admirable *Vindication of his Appendix*, in the summer of the same year, left the believers in this daring imposture nothing but 'the resolution to say again what had been said before.' [M.]

misery, that I cannot but earnestly enjoin you to avoid it. Live on what you have; live if you can on less; do not borrow either for vanity or pleasure; the vanity will end in shame, and the pleasure in regret.' . . . . 'Do not accustom yourself to consider debt only as an inconvenience; you will find it a calamity. Poverty takes away so many means of doing good, and produces so much inability to resist evil, both natural and moral, that it is by all virtuous means to be avoided. Consider a man whose fortune is very narrow; whatever be his rank by birth, or whatever his reputation by intellectual excellence, what good can he do? or what evil can he prevent? That he cannot help the needy is evident; he has nothing to spare. But, perhaps, his advice or admonition may be useful. His poverty will destroy his influence: many more can find that he is poor, than that he is wise; and few will reverence the understanding that is of so little advantage to its owner. I say nothing of the personal wretchedness of a debtor, which, however, has passed into a proverb. Of riches, it is not necessary to write the praise. Let it, however, be remembered, that he who has money to spare, has it always in his power to benefit others; and of such power a good man must always be desirous. . . . .

'Your œconomy, I suppose, begins now to be settled; your expences are adjusted to your revenue, and all your people in their proper places. Resolve not to be poor: whatever you have, spend less. Poverty is a great enemy to human happiness; it certainly destroys liberty, and it makes some virtues impracticable, and others extremely difficult.'

186. *Conversation* [1783].

Talking of conversation, he said, 'There must, in the first place, be knowledge, there must be materials;—in the second place, there must be a command of words;—in the third place, there must be imagination, to place things in such views as they are not commonly seen in;—and in the fourth place, there must be presence of mind, and a resolution that is not to be overcome by failures: this last is an essential requisite; for want of it many people do not excel in conversation. Now *I* want it: I throw up the game upon losing a trick.' I wondered to hear him talk thus of himself, and said, ' I don't know, Sir, how this may be; but I am sure you beat other people's cards out of their hands.' I doubt whether he heard this remark. While he went on talking triumphantly, I was fixed in admiration, and said to Mrs. Thrale, ' O, for short-hand to take this down!' 'You'll carry it all in your head, (said she;) a long head is as good as short-hand.'

187. *Burke's Talk* [1783].

'Burke's talk is the ebullition of his mind; he does not talk from a desire of distinction, but because his mind is full.'

188. *Truth and Fiction* [1783].

Talking of an acquaintance of ours, whose narratives, which abounded in curious and interesting topicks, were unhappily found to be very fábulous; I mentioned Lord Mansfield's having said to me, 'Suppose we believe one *half* of what he tells.' JOHNSON. 'Ay; but we don't know *which* half to believe. By his lying we lose not only our reverence for him, but all comfort in his conversation.' BOSWELL. 'May we not take it as amusing fiction?' JOHNSON. 'Sir, the misfortune is, that you will insensibly believe as much of it as you incline to believe.'

189. *Inculto sub Corpore* [1783].

On the frame of his portrait, Mr. Beauclerk had inscribed,—

'———— *Ingenium ingens*
Inculto latet hoc sub corpore.'

After Mr. Beauclerk's death, when it became Mr. Langton's property, he made the inscription be defaced. Johnson said complacently, 'It was kind in you to take it off;' and then after a short pause, added, 'and not unkind in him to put it on.'

190. *Dexterity in Retort* [1783].

Johnson's dexterity in retort, when he seemed to be driven to an extremity by his adversary, was very remarkable. Of his power in this respect, our common friend, Mr. Windham, of Norfolk, has been pleased to furnish me with an eminent instance. However unfavourable to Scotland, he uniformly gave liberal praise to George Buchanan, as a writer. In a conversation concerning the literary merits of the two countries, in which Buchanan was introduced, a Scotchman, imagining that on this ground he should have an undoubted triumph over him, exclaimed, 'Ah, Dr. Johnson, what would you have said of Buchanan, had he been an Englishman?'—'Why, Sir, (said Johnson, after a little pause,) I should *not* have said of Buchanan, had he been an *Englishman*, what I will now say of him as a *Scotchman*,—that he was the only man of genius his country ever produced.'

191. *Maurice Morgann* [1783].

Maurice Morgann, Esq., authour of the very ingenious *Essay on the character of Falstaff*[1], being a particular friend of his Lordship, had once an opportunity of entertaining Johnson for a day or two at Wickham, when its Lord was absent, and by him I have been favoured with two anecdotes.

One is not a little to the credit of Johnson's candour. Mr. Morgann and he had a dispute pretty late at night, in which Johnson would not give up, though he had the wrong side, and in short, both kept the field. Next morning, when they met in the breakfasting-room, Dr. Johnson accosted Mr. Morgann thus: 'Sir, I have been thinking on our dispute last night—*You were in the right.*'

The other was as follows: Johnson, for sport perhaps, or from the spirit of contradiction, eagerly maintained that Derrick had merit as a writer. Mr. Morgann argued with him directly, in vain. At length he had

[1] Johnson being asked his opinion of this Essay, answered, 'Why, Sir, we shall have the man come forth again; and as he has proved Falstaff to be no coward, he may prove Iago to be a very good character.'

recourse to this device. 'Pray, Sir, (said he,) whether do you reckon Derrick or Smart the best poet?' Johnson at once felt himself rouzed; and answered, 'Sir, there is no settling the point of precedency between a louse and a flea.'

192. *Johnson's Kindness* [1783].

Johnson's love of little children, which he discovered upon all occasions, calling them 'pretty dears,' and giving them sweetmeats, was an undoubted proof of the real humanity and gentleness of his disposition. His uncommon kindness to his servants, and serious concern, not only for their comfort in this world, but their happiness in the next, was another unquestionable evidence of what all, who were intimately acquainted with him, knew to be true.

Nor would it be just, under this head, to omit the fondness which he shewed for animals which he had taken under his protection. I never shall forget the indulgence with which he treated Hodge, his cat; for whom he himself used to go out and buy oysters, lest the servants having that trouble should take a dislike to the poor creature. I am, unluckily, one of those who have an antipathy to a cat, so that I am uneasy when in the room with one; and I own, I frequently suffered a good deal from the presence of this same Hodge. I recollect him one day scrambling up Dr. Johnson's breast, apparently with much satisfaction, while my friend smiling and half-whistling, rubbed down his back, and pulled him by the tail; and when I observed he was a fine cat, saying, 'Why yes, Sir, but I have had cats whom I liked better than this;' and then as if perceiving Hodge to be out of countenance, adding, 'but he is a very fine cat, a very fine cat indeed.'

193. *Publick Affairs* [1783].

BOSWELL. 'I wish much to be in Parliament, Sir.' JOHNSON. 'Why, Sir, unless you come resolved to support any administration, you would be the worse for being in Parliament, because you would be obliged to live more expensively.'—BOSWELL. 'Perhaps, Sir, I should be the less happy for being in Parliament. I never would sell my vote, and I should be vexed if things went wrong.' JOHNSON. 'That's cant, Sir. It would not vex you more in the house, than in the gallery: publick affairs vex no man.' BOSWELL. 'Have not they vexed yourself a little, Sir? Have not you been vexed by all the turbulence of this reign, and by that absurd vote of the House of Commons, "That the influence of the Crown has increased, is increasing, and ought to be diminished?"' JOHNSON. 'Sir, I have never slept an hour less, nor eat an ounce less meat. I would have knocked the factious dogs on the head, to be sure; but I was not *vexed*.' BOSWELL. 'I declare, Sir, upon my honour, I did imagine I was vexed, and took a pride in it; but it *was*, perhaps, cant; for I own I neither ate less, nor slept less.' JOHNSON. 'My dear friend, clear your *mind* of cant. You may *talk* as other people do: you may say to a man, "Sir, I am your most humble servant." You are *not* his most humble servant. You may say, "These are bad times; it is a melancholy thing to be reserved to such times." You don't mind the times. You tell a man, "I am sorry you had such bad weather the last day of your journey, and were so much wet." You don't care six-pence whether he is wet or dry. You may *talk* in this manner; it is a mode of talking in Society: but don't *think* foolishly.'

194. *Mrs. Siddons* [1783].

He this autumn received a visit from the celebrated Mrs. Siddons. . . . .

Mr. Kemble has favoured me with the following minute of what passed at this visit.

'When Mrs. Siddons came into the room, there happened to be no chair ready for her, which he observing, said with a smile, "Madam, you who so often occasion a want of seats to other people, will the more easily excuse the want of one yourself."

'Having placed himself by her, he with great good humour entered upon a consideration of the English drama; and, among other inquiries, particularly asked her which of Shakspeare's characters she was most pleased with. Upon her answering that she thought the character of Queen Catharine, in *Henry the Eighth,* the most natural :—" I think so too, Madam; (said he;) and whenever you perform it, I will once more hobble out to the theatre myself." Mrs. Siddons promised she would do herself the honour of acting his favourite part for him; but many circumstances happened to prevent the representation of *King Henry the Eighth* during the Doctor's life.'

195. *Burke's Talk* [1784].

BOSWELL. 'Mr. Burke has a constant stream of conversation.' JOHNSON. 'Yes, Sir; if a man were to go by chance at the same time with Burke under a shed, to shun a shower, he would say—"this is an extraordinary man." If Burke should go into a stable to see his horse drest, the ostler would say—"we have had an extraordinary man here."'

196. *Collecting Books* [1784].

He said, he thought it unnecessary to collect many editions of a book, which were all the same, except as to the paper and print; he would have the original, and all the translations, and all the editions which had any variations in the text. He approved of the famous collection of editions of Horace by Douglas, mentioned by Pope, who is said to have had a closet filled with them; and he added, 'every man should try to collect one book in that manner, and present it to a publick library.'

197. *Weak-nerved People* [1784].

He however charged Mr. Langton with what he thought want of judgement upon an interesting occasion. 'When I was ill, (said he) I desired he would tell me sincerely in what he thought my life was faulty. Sir, he brought me a sheet of paper, on which he had written down several texts of Scripture, recommending christian charity. And when I questioned him what occasion I had given for such an

animadversion, all that he could say amounted to this,
—that I sometimes contradicted people in conversation.
Now what harm does it do to any man to be contradicted?' BOSWELL. 'I suppose he meant the
manner of doing it; roughly,—and harshly.' JOHNSON.
'And who is the worse for that?' BOSWELL. 'It
hurts people of weak nerves.' JOHNSON. 'I know no
such weak-nerved people.' Mr. Burke, to whom I
related this conference, said, 'It is well, if when a man
comes to die, he has nothing heavier upon his conscience
than having been a little rough in conversation.'

Johnson, at the time when the paper was presented
to him, though at first pleased with the attention of his
friend, whom he thanked in an earnest manner, soon
exclaimed, in a loud and angry tone, 'What is your
drift, Sir?' Sir Joshua Reynolds pleasantly observed,
that it was a scene for a comedy, to see a penitent get
into a violent passion and belabour his confessor.

198. *Carve Heads upon Cherry-Stones* [1784].

Mrs. Kennicot related, in his presence, a lively saying of Dr. Johnson to Miss Hannah More, who had
expressed a wonder that the poet who had written
Paradise Lost should write such poor Sonnets:—
'Milton, Madam, was a genius that could cut a Colossus
from a rock; but could not carve heads upon cherry-
stones.'

199. *Argument and Understanding* [1784].

Johnson having argued for some time with a pertina-
cious gentleman; his opponent, who had talked in a
very puzzling manner, happened to say, 'I don't under-

stand you, Sir:' upon which Johnson observed, 'Sir, I have found you an argument; but I am not obliged to find you an understanding.'

200. *The Rehearsal* [1784].

He seemed to take a pleasure in speaking in his own style; for when he had carelessly missed it, he would repeat the thought translated into it. Talking of the Comedy of *The Rehearsal*, he said, 'It has not wit enough to keep it sweet.' This was easy;—he therefore caught himself, and pronounced a more round sentence; 'It has not vitality enough to preserve it from putrefaction.'

201. *Application to Lord Thurlow* [1784].

The anxiety of his friends to preserve so estimable a life, as long as human means might be supposed to have influence, made them plan for him a retreat from the severity of a British winter, to the mild climate of Italy. This scheme was at last brought to a serious resolution at General Paoli's, where I had often talked of it. One essential matter, however, I understood was necessary to be previously settled, which was obtaining such an addition to his income, as would be sufficient to enable him to defray the expence in a manner becoming the first literary character of a great nation, and, independent of all his other merits, the Authour of THE DICTIONARY OF THE ENGLISH LANGUAGE. The person to whom I above all others thought I should apply to negociate this business, was the Lord Chancellor [1], because I knew that he highly valued Johnson, and that Johnson highly valued his Lordship; so that it was no degradation of my illustrious friend to solicit for him the favour of such a man. . . . .

I first consulted with Sir Joshua Reynolds, who perfectly coincided in opinion with me; and I therefore, though personally very little known to his Lordship, wrote to him, stating the case, and requesting his good offices for Dr. Johnson. I mentioned that I was obliged to set out for Scotland early in the following week, so that if his Lordship should have any commands for me as to this pious negociation, he would be pleased to send them before that time; otherwise Sir Joshua Reynolds would give all attention to it.

202. *The Same* [1784].

On Monday, June 28, I had the honour to receive from the Lord Chancellor the following letter:

'To James Boswell, Esq.

'Sir,—I should have answered your letter immediately; if, (being much engaged when I received it) I had not put it in my pocket, and forgot to open it till this morning.

'I am much obliged to you for the suggestion; and I will adopt and press it as far as I can. The best argument, I am sure, and I hope it is not likely to fail, is Dr. Johnson's merit. But it will be necessary, if I

[1] Edward Lord Thurlow.

should be so unfortunate as to miss seeing you, to converse with Sir Joshua on the sum it will be proper to ask,—in short, upon the means of setting him out. It would be a reflection on us all, if such a man should perish for want of the means to take care of his health. Yours, &c. 'THURLOW.'

This letter gave me a very high satisfaction; I next day went and shewed it to Sir Joshua Reynolds, who was exceedingly pleased with it. He thought that I should now communicate the negociation to Dr. Johnson, who might afterwards complain if the attention with which he had been honoured, should be too long concealed from him. I intended to set out for Scotland next morning; but Sir Joshua cordially insisted that I should stay another day, that Johnson and I might dine with him, that we three might talk of his Italian Tour, and, as Sir Joshua expressed himself, 'have it all out.' I hastened to Johnson, and was told by him that he was rather better to-day. BOSWELL. 'I am very anxious about you, Sir, and particularly that you should go to Italy for the winter, which I believe is your own wish.' JOHNSON. 'It is, Sir.' BOSWELL. 'You have no objection, I presume, but the money it would require.' JOHNSON. 'Why, no, Sir.'—Upon which I gave him a particular account of what had been done, and read to him the Lord Chancellor's letter.—He listened with much attention; then warmly said, 'This is taking prodigious pains about a man.'—'O! Sir, (said I, with most sincere affection,) your friends would do every thing for you.' He paused,—

grew more and more agitated,—till tears started into his eyes, and he exclaimed with fervent emotion, 'GOD bless you all.' I was so affected that I also shed tears.— After a short silence, he renewed and extended his grateful benediction, 'GOD bless you all, for JESUS CHRIST'S sake.' We both remained for some time unable to speak.—He rose suddenly and quitted the room, quite melted in tenderness. He staid but a short time, till he had recovered his firmness; soon after he returned I left him, having first engaged him to dine at Sir Joshua Reynolds's, next day.—I never was again under that roof which I had so long reverenced.

On Wednesday, June 30, the friendly confidential dinner with Sir Joshua Reynolds took place, no other company being present. Had I known that this was the last time that I should enjoy in this world, the conversation of a friend whom I so much respected, and from whom I derived so much instruction and entertainment, I should have been deeply affected. When I now look back to it, I am vexed that a single word should have been forgotten.

Both Sir Joshua and I were so sanguine in our expectations, that we expatiated with confidence on the liberal provision which we were sure would be made for him, conjecturing whether munificence would be displayed in one large donation, or in an ample increase of his pension. He himself catched so much of our enthusiasm, as to allow himself to suppose it not impossible that our hopes might in one way or other be realised. He said that he would rather have his pension doubled than a grant of a thousand pounds;

'For, (said he,) though probably I may not live to receive as much as a thousand pounds, a man would have the consciousness that he should pass the remainder of his life in splendour, how long soever it might be.' Considering what a moderate proportion an income of six hundred pounds a year bears to innumerable fortunes in this country, it is worthy of remark, that a man so truly great should think it splendour.

203. *Johnson's and Boswell's Last Meeting* [1784].

I accompanied him in Sir Joshua Reynolds's coach, to the entry of Bolt-court. He asked me whether I would not go with him to his house; I declined it, from an apprehension that my spirits would sink. We bade adieu to each other affectionately in the carriage. When he had got down upon the foot-pavement, he called out, 'Fare you well;' and without looking back, sprung away with a kind of pathetick briskness, if I may use that expression, which seemed to indicate a struggle to conceal uneasiness, and impressed me with a foreboding of our long, long separation.

204. *The Balloon* [1784. *Letters to Dr. Brocklesby and Sir Joshua Reynolds*].

'Is this the balloon that has been so long expected, this balloon to which I subscribed, but without payment? It is pity that philosophers have been disappointed, and shame that they have been cheated; but I know not well how to prevent either. Of this experiment I have read nothing; where was it exhibited? and who was the man that ran away with so much money? Continue, dear Sir, to write often and more at a time; for none of your prescriptions operate to their proper uses more certainly than your letters operate as cordials.' . . . .

'On one day I had three letters about the air-balloon: yours was far the best, and has enabled me to impart to my friends in the country an idea of this species of amusement. . . . .'

'The fate of the balloon I do not much lament: to make new balloons, is to repeat the jest again. We now know a method of mounting into the air, and, I think, are not likely to know more. The vehicles can serve no use till we can guide them; and they can gratify no curiosity till we mount with them to greater heights than we can reach without; till we rise above the tops of the highest mountains, which we have yet not done. We know the state of the air in all its regions, to the top of Teneriffe, and therefore, learn nothing from those who navigate a balloon below the clouds. The first experiment, however, was bold, and deserved applause and reward. But since it has been performed, and its event is known, I had rather now find a medicine that can ease an asthma.' . . . .

'I have three letters this day, all about the balloon, I could have been content with one. Do not write about the balloon, whatever else you may think proper to say.'

205. *Johnson's Last Days* [1784].

During his last illness, Johnson experienced the steady and kind attachment of his numerous friends. Mr. Hoole has drawn up a narrative of what passed in the visits which he paid him during that time, from the 10th of November to the 13th of December, the day of his death, inclusive, and has favoured me with a perusal of it, with permission to make extracts, which I have done. Nobody was more attentive to him than Mr. Langton, to whom he tenderly said, *Te teneam moriens deficiente manu.* And I think it highly to the honour of Mr. Windham, that his important occupations as an active statesman did not prevent him from paying assiduous respect to the dying Sage whom he revered. Mr. Langton informs me, that, 'one day he found Mr. Burke and four or five more friends sitting with Johnson. Mr. Burke said to him, " I am afraid, Sir, such a number of us may be oppressive to you." " No, Sir, (said Johnson,) it is not so; and I must be in a wretched state, indeed, when your company would not be a delight to me." Mr. Burke, in a tremulous voice, expressive of being very tenderly affected, replied, " My dear Sir, you have always been too good to me." Immediately afterwards he went away. This was the last circumstance in the acquaintance of these two eminent men.'

206. *His Epitaph* [1784].

A few days before his death, he had asked Sir John Hawkins, as one of his executors, where he should be buried; and on being answered, 'Doubtless, in Westminster-Abbey,' seemed to feel a satisfaction, very natural to a Poet; and indeed in my opinion very natural to every man of any imagination, who has no family sepulchre in which he can be laid with his fathers. Accordingly, upon Monday, December 20, his remains were deposited in that noble and renowned edifice; and over his grave was placed a large blue flag-stone, with this inscription :—

'SAMUEL JOHNSON, LL.D.

Obiit XIII *die Decembris,*

Anno Domini

M.DCC.LXXXIV.

Ætatis suæ LXXV.'

207. *Johnson is Dead* [1784].

I trust, I shall not be accused of affectation, when I declare, that I find myself unable to express all that I felt upon the loss of such a 'Guide, Philosopher, and Friend.' I shall, therefore, not say one word of my own, but adopt those of an eminent friend[1], which he uttered with an abrupt felicity, superior to all studied compositions :—' He has made a chasm, which not only nothing can fill up, but which nothing has a tendency to fill up.—Johnson is dead.—Let us go to the next best :—there is nobody ;—no man can be said to put you in mind of Johnson.'

[1] The late Right Hon. William Gerrard Hamilton. [M.]

2142 O

208. *Boswell's Conclusion* [1784].

Such was SAMUEL JOHNSON, a man whose talents, acquirements, and virtues, were so extraordinary, that the more his character is considered, the more he will be regarded by the present age, and by posterity, with admiration and reverence.

EDITOR'S NOTES

EDITOR'S NOTES

The references are to the numbers of the extracts.

1. *Quo fit ut omnis* : ' The whole life of the Old Man lies open to our view, as if it were painted on a votive picture '. (Horace, *Satires* ii. 1. 33.)

2. *Sir Joshua Reynolds* (1723-92 : President of the Royal Academy), whom, echoing the affectionate familiarity of his contemporaries, we still call plain ' Sir Joshua '. For his portraits of Johnson see 25, 189.

Reynolds's *Discourses* on painting, addressed to the Royal Academy, are still regarded as a classic of criticism. The first seven Discourses, delivered 1769–76, were republished in 1778 with a Dedication to the King written by Johnson.

noctes cœnaeque deûm: literally, ' nights and banquets of the gods '. (Horace, *Satires* ii. 6. 65.)

3. Carlyle called Boswell's book a *Johnsoniad.*

Quid virtus: ' To shew what wisdom and what sense can do,
The poet sets Ulysses in our view '.
(Horace, *Epistles* i. 2. 17.)

Auchinleck: pronounced Affléck, as Boswell informs us.

4. *I am not vain enough.* Yet (writes Macaulay) ' Boswell is the first of biographers. . . . *Eclipse* is first, the rest nowhere.'

he will be seen more completely. The claim is amply justified. We know indefinitely more of Johnson than we know of Socrates, or Julius Caesar, or Erasmus ; more than we know even of Napoleon, or Charles Lamb, or Thackeray. This we owe almost entirely to Boswell.

5. *booksellers' shops.* The booksellers' shops were centres of literature. The bookseller was also the publisher, and new books sought their public across the counter.

6. *Dr. Taylor:* the Rev. Dr. Taylor of Ashbourne in Derbyshire, Johnson's schoolfellow and friend. Johnson and Boswell were his guests at Ashbourne in 1776 and 1777.

7. *Bentley:* Richard Bentley (1662–1742) of Cambridge, author of the Dissertations *Upon the Epistles of Phalaris* (1697 and 1699), and the most famous of English Greek scholars.

Smith: Adam Smith (1723-90) of the University of Glasgow, author of *The Wealth of Nations.*

8. Quoted from the character of Gilbert Walmsley, an early friend of Johnson, which occurs in the life of Edmund Smith in the *Lives of the Poets.*

eclipsed the gaiety of nations. See 163.

12. *The debates in Parliament:* the art of shorthand reporting was in its infancy.

13. *London: LONDON, A Poem, in imitation of the Third Satire of Juvenal* (May 1738).

Marmor Norfolciense: ' In this performance, he, in a feigned inscription, supposed to have been found in Norfolk, the county of Sir Robert Walpole, then the obnoxious prime minister of this country, inveighs against the Brunswick succession. . . . To this supposed prophecy he added a Commentary, making each expression apply to the times, with warm anti-Hanoverian zeal.' (Boswell.)

my L^d gore: Earl Gower (pronounced *Gore*), on Pope's application, had tried to procure a Dublin degree for Johnson by using the influence of his friends with Dean Swift.

14. Johnson's *Dictionary* was for nearly a century an indispensable part of every domestic library. It is now in many ways obsolete ; the cheapest modern dictionaries (profiting by the information available in more elaborate works) give more words and more scientific etymologies. But Johnson's book should be in the hands of every student of his time or of the times of Dryden and Pope. The definitions are masterly ; and Malone observes that ' so happily selected are the greater part of the examples in that incomparable work, that if the most striking passages found in it were collected by one of our modern book-makers, under the title of *The Beauties of Johnson's Dictionary,* they would form a very pleasing and popular volume.' The preface is a masterpiece.

his brother Robert's shop. ' The worthy, modest, and ingenious Mr. Robert Dodsley' (Boswell) ' raised himself from the station of a footman' and became the most famous book-seller of his century. He is best remembered for his *Collection of Poems in six volumes by several hands* (1748-58), often mentioned by Boswell, and for his *Select Collection of Old Plays* (1744), which Charles Lamb loved so well.

16. *Topham Beauclerk* was a great-grandson of Charles II.

17. *Lord Chesterfield*: Philip Dormer Stanhope, fourth Earl of Chesterfield, the most accomplished fine gentleman of his time ; of whose *Letters* to his natural son Johnson said 'they teach the morals of a whore, and the manners of a dancing master'. See 68.

The shepherd in Virgil: Eclogue viii. 43 'nunc scio quid sit Amor,' 'I know thee, Love ! in deserts thou wast hid'. (Dryden's translation.)

19. Johnson reviewing Hanway's *Essay on Tea* in the *Literary Magazine* informed his readers that ' Tea was first imported from *Holland* by the earls of *Arlington* and *Ossory*, in 1666 ; from their ladies the women of quality learned its use.' But Samuel Pepys on 28 Sept. 1660 ' did send for a cup of tee (a China drink) of which I never had drank before.'

20. This charming sentence is a good illustration of what happens when Johnson uses the sledgehammer of his style to crack a nut.

21. Welsh and Irish (as also Gaelic or Erse, Breton, and Corn-ish) are closely akin. The Basque language is quite different.

22. *Warburton*: William Warburton (1698-1779), Bishop of Gloucester ; the friend of Pope and editor of Shakespeare.

Theobald: Lewis Theobald, another editor of Shakespeare, and author of some famous emendations of Shakespeare's text.

Dr. Charles Burney (1757-1817), known for his *History of Music*, and still better known as Johnson's friend and as the amiable father of Johnson's favourite Fanny Burney (who married a French emigrant and became Madame D'Arblay), authoress of *Evelina, Cecilia*, and the famous *Diary*.

Dr. Warton: the Rev. Dr. Thomas Warton (1728-90), Professor of Poetry at Oxford and afterwards Poet Laureate ; one of Johnson's intimate friends. The *Observations on the*

Faerie Queene of Spenser and the *History of English Poetry* are his chief critical works.   His brother Joseph (1722–1800) was Head Master of Winchester, and author of an *Essay on the Writings and Genius of Pope.*

23. This letter was not printed in Boswell's lifetime, but was added by Malone to the fourth edition.

25. *Mr. Thomas Davies* was a humble member of the circle. He was an unsuccessful though an enterprising bookseller, and went bankrupt.   He was more successful with his *Memoirs of David Garrick,* of which Johnson wrote: 'Mr. Davies has got great success as an authour, generated by the corruption of a bookseller'.

26. *Christopher Smart* (1722–71).   His best-known poem is the *Song to David,* written in madness.

29. *Mallet:* David Malloch (1705?–65), a Scotchman who learned to speak English without an accent, and 'inclined to disencumber himself from all adherences of his original, took upon him to change his name from Scotch *Malloch* to English *Mallet*' (Johnson, *Life of Mallet*).   He was the friend of Thomson, the author of the *Seasons,* with whom he collaborated, and a not unsuccessful dramatist.

30. Boswell's character of Goldsmith seems to be perfectly candid ; though it may make us think of a character of Charles Lamb that might have been written by Tom Moore.   After Lamb, Goldsmith is perhaps the most amiable creature among English writers : he was also 'a very great man'.   But his contemporaries are unanimous in the opinion that he was an absurd person, and they can hardly have been wrong ; though it is true that some of the sayings which they quote in proof of his absurdity are pieces of Irish humour which they wholly failed to appreciate. It seems unlikely that the severe things which Boswell says of Goldsmith (most of them are quoted from Johnson, who loved him) were prompted by envy.   'Honest Dr. Goldsmith' did not move in the exalted circles in which it was Boswell's ambition to shine : and if he had been envious of any one on the score of intimacy with Johnson, we should expect him to vent his spleen on Burke and Beauclerk rather than on Goldsmith.

The best book on Goldsmith, and one of the best accounts of the Johnsonian circle, is the life by John Forster, who wrote also the life of Dickens. Forster made an abridgement of his larger work, which was published in 1855, and has been reprinted.

Oliver Goldsmith (1728-74) is most famous for his *Vicar of Wakefield* (1766; see 31), his two poems *The Traveller* (1765; see 72, 142) and *The Deserted Village* (1770: Johnson's contributions to both are discussed by Boswell under the year 1766; see 72), and the two comedies *The Good-Natured Man*, (1768; Johnson wrote the Prologue) and *She Stoops to Conquer* (1773; see 66). His *Histories* of England and Rome and his *Animated Nature* contain passages written as only Goldsmith could write; but he knew little of history, and less of natural science. In 1759 Goldsmith produced a weekly periodical *The Bee*, which was published as a volume (*The Bee. Being Essays on the Most Interesting Subjects*) in the same year. *The Citizen of the World; or, Letters from a Chinese Philosopher, residing in London, to his Friend in the East*, appeared in the *The Public Ledger* in 1760 and 1761, and separately in 1762. The essays in *The Bee*, and some others, were reprinted in 1765 under the title *Essays. By Oliver Goldsmith*; in the preface to this volume he confesses that his essays ' shared the common fate, without assisting the bookseller's aims, or extending the writer's reputation. The public were too strenuously employed with their own follies, to be assiduous in estimating mine.'

The best edition of Goldsmith's poems is Mr. Austin Dobson's very entertaining volume in the *Oxford Poets*. Of *The Vicar* and the plays there are numberless reprints.

35. *The King of Prussia*: Frederick the Great. ' His conversation is like that of other men upon common topicks, his letters have an air of familiar elegance, and his whole conduct is that of a man who has to do with men, and who is not ignorant what motives will prevail over friends or enemies.' Johnson, Essay on *The King of Prussia* (contributed to the *Literary Magazine*, 1756).

37. *Martin*: Martin Martin's *Description of the Western Islands of Scotland* (1703).

39. *Mr. Thomas Sheridan :* generally 'Old Mr. Sheridan' to distinguish him from his more famous son Richard, the author of *The School for Scandal* and *The Rivals*, which Johnson called 'the two best comedies of his age'. Thomas Sheridan gave lectures on elocution.

47. Johnson was greatly attached to the Thrales, and with the lady he kept up a lively correspondence. After her husband's death in 1781 Mrs. Thrale grew weary of Johnson. Boswell says (1782), 'as her vanity had been fully gratified, by having the Colossus of Literature attached to her for many years, she gradually became less assiduous to please him.' Mrs. Thrale says : 'Veneration for his virtue, reverence for his talents, delight in his conversation, and habitual endurance of a yoke my husband first put upon me, and of which he contentedly bore his share for sixteen or seventeen years, made me go on so long with Mr. Johnson ; but the perpetual confinement I will own to have been terrifying in the first years of our friendship, and irksome in the last ; nor could I pretend to support it without help, when my coadjutor was no more' (*Anecdotes :* quoted by Boswell under 1784). Finally in 1784 she disgraced herself in the eyes of the world by becoming engaged to 'Signor Piozzi, an Italian musick-master'.

Mrs. Piozzi published in 1786 *Anecdotes of the late Samuel Johnson* and in 1788 *Letters to and from the late Samuel Johnson.* Johnson often rebuked her for 'laxity of narration' ; and Boswell frequently protests against the neglect or distortion of truth shown in her *Anecdotes*.

49. *The planters of America.* See 134 and note.

51. *conglobulate.* See 74 for the migration of woodcock. The migration of birds was long received with incredulity. Even so great a naturalist as White of Selborne held out for the hibernation of swallows. Swallows were seen gathering near pools, and it was supposed they took refuge under water.

52. Boswell made himself ridiculous by talking too much of his travels in Corsica and his friendship with General Paoli, and earned the nickname of 'Corsica Boswell'.

54. *Brighthelmstone :* Brighton.

56. *Mrs. Montagu* is now less distinguished by her Essay on

Shakespeare than by her having been the first of the Blue-stockings. See 180.

Du Bos and Bouhours : the Abbé Du Bos and Père Dominique Bouhours were critical writers whose books were translated into English and had an important influence. The English version of Bouhours appeared in 1705: *The Art of Criticism, or the Method of making a Right Judgment upon Subjects of Wit and Learning* ; of Du Bos in 1748 : *Critical Reflections on Poetry, Painting, and Music. Translated into English by Thomas Nugent, Gent.*

57. 'Is it not easy to imagine the scene? The pleasant, excitable, insistent voice of Boswell—"With regard to death, Sir "; Johnson's brief, wise verdict, and dismissal of the topic ; Boswell's mosquito-like return, and Johnson's outburst of wrath. It was not death that he feared; it was Boswell on death.' Raleigh, *Essays on Johnson.*

61. *Mallet.* See 29 n.

62. If Johnson was not merely 'talking for victory'; if it was his considered opinion that the contemporaries of Demosthenes and Cicero were barbarians (and he repeated it, see 67) it is charitable to suppose that he had in mind the institution of slavery. But the speeches of Demosthenes were not addressed to slaves.

64. *Lord Mansfield :* William Murray, first Earl of Mansfield, who became Lord Chief Justice of England ; one of Pope's noble friends.

66. *Dr. Beattie :* James Beattie (1735-1803) Professor of Moral Philosophy at Aberdeen and author of *The Minstrel.*

Great Dictionary means the large work ; Johnson had published also an abridgement.

Baretti : Joseph Baretti, not the least remarkable member of the Johnsonian circle. He came to London from Italy in 1750. He gave lessons in Italian, and was for some years attached to the Thrale family as tutor to Miss Thrale. He was a man of violent and capricious temper, and after his quarrel with Mrs. Thrale made a brutal attack on her in the *European Magazine.* His copies of her *Anecdotes* and *Letters* have been preserved, and his marginal comments have been found valuable by biographers. Neither he nor Mrs. Thrale can be trusted to tell the truth, but their versions correct each other.

Baretti was intimate with Johnson, who had a regard for him. He wrote the dedication of his *Italian and English Dictionary*, which long remained a standard work.

Davies. See 25 n.

A new comedy: She Stoops to Conquer.

72. *Robertson:* Dr. William Robertson (1721-93), Principal of the University of Edinburgh; author of a *History of Scotland* and a *History of America*, which had a great vogue.

Vertot: René Vertot (1655-1735), a popular French historian. His *Histoire des révolutions romaines* was translated by John Ozell; the translation was published in 1720.

a Natural History: Animated Nature.

73. *Edmund Burke* (1729-97). Burke's political writings and career are not often mentioned in Boswell; but as a brilliant talker he is often quoted. See Index.

74. See 51.

exceptio probat regulam. The full formula is *exceptio probat regulam in casibus non exceptis*—a maxim of Roman Law: 'the exception proves the rule *in the cases not excepted*'. Thus 'it is lawful to shoot a burglar if he is armed' implies that it is *not* lawful to shoot burglars in general; the *exception* of the armed burglar *proves the rule* about unarmed burglars. This famous phrase, which Johnson applies correctly, is constantly misused, as if it meant that the exception proves the rule to which it is an exception; as if the existence of a white crow could prove that crows are black—which is absurd.

75. *the ten persecutions:* of the early Christian Church.

77. *Literary Property.* The Act of Queen Anne gave protection of twenty-one years to books already published, and for fourteen years to books subsequently published, with a second term of fourteen years if the author should be still alive. There was also a supposed common-law right of Literary Property; 'it has always been understood by the *trade*, that he, who buys the copyright of a book from the authour, obtains a perpetual property' (Johnson, quoted by Boswell, 1763). This supposed

right was quashed by a decision of the House of Lords. Johnson was not in favour of perpetual copyright, but thought the term should be increased from fourteen years to sixty.

The Act of 1842 made the term forty-two years (or seven years after the author's death, whichever were the longer). The Act which came into force in 1912 made it fifty years after the author's death.

78. Johnson's and Boswell's tour in Scotland produced two notable books; Johnson's *Journey to the Western Islands of Scotland* (1775 ; 'that most ceremonious of diaries '—Raleigh) and Boswell's *Journal of a Tour to the Hebrides*, which, though not published till 1785, after Johnson's death, was read in manuscript by Johnson, Mrs. Thrale (Boswell, 1775), and others.

79. ' My wife was so good as to devote the greater part of the morning to the endless task of pouring out tea for my friend and his visitors ' (*Tour to the Hebrides*).

80. *To come to Jona.* See 131.

81. *Chambers . . . is gone far :* to India, where he became a judge and Sir Robert Chambers.

82. *Ossian.* James Macpherson published *Fragments of Ancient Poetry collected in the Highlands of Scotland* (Edinburgh, 1760) and *Fingal, an ancient epic poem* (London, 1762). A furious controversy raged over these books ; most Englishmen, following Johnson, denounced them for impudent forgeries; almost all Scotsmen 'conspired' to proclaim them genuine. That they were forgeries is now agreed, but the book had greater merit than Johnson allowed it.

Dr. Blair : Hugh Blair (1718-1800), of Edinburgh, author of the famous *Sermons*, which were first published on Johnson's warm recommendation. Blair was not only one of the ministers of the High Church in Edinburgh, but also Professor of Rhetoric and Belles Lettres in the University. His *Lectures on Rhetoric and Belles Lettres*, published in two handsome quartos in 1783, were for long popular and influential. Blair believed in the authenticity of *Ossian*, and in his *Critical Dissertation* wrote of one episode in the poem, ' I know no passage more sublime in the writings of any uninspired author '.

De non existentibus : ' what cannot be produced is held not to exist.'

85. *Gray* : Thomas Gray (1716-71). His poems are best read in the collected edition published in his lifetime: POEMS BY Mr. GRAY. LONDON : Printed for J. DODSLEY, in Pall-Mall. (1768 ; reprinted in *Oxford Library of Prose and Poetry*.) Modern critical editions give the numerous variations in the text. Johnson often spoke slightingly of Gray's poems ; and his *Life of Gray*, which Macaulay called ' the very worst' of the *Lives*, betrays a lack of sympathy with the poet and his poems. ' By some violent Whigs', says Boswell, ' he was arraigned of injustice to Milton ; by some Cambridge men of depreciating Gray'. Yet it must not be forgotten that the *Life of Gray* concludes with noble praise of the *Elegy* :

' In the character of his Elegy I rejoice to concur with the common reader ; for by the common sense of readers uncorrupted with literary prejudices, after all the refinements of subtilty and the dogmatism of learning, must be finally decided all claim to poetical honours. The *Church-yard* abounds with images which find a mirrour in every mind, and with sentiments to which every bosom returns an echo. The four stanzas beginning *Yet even these bones*, are to me original : I have never seen the notions in any other place ; yet he that reads them here, persuades himself that he has always felt them. Had Gray written often thus, it had been vain to blame, and useless to praise him.'

87. Lord North was the Chancellor of the University.

88. *Mrs. Williams* was the most notable of the retainers whom Johnson kept in his house and in part maintained. ' Mrs. Anna Williams, daughter of a very ingenious Welsh physician, and a woman of more than ordinary talents and literature, having come to London in hopes of being cured of a cataract in both her eyes, which afterwards ended in total blindness, was kindly received as a constant visitor at his house while Mrs. Johnson lived ; and after her death . . . she had an apartment from him during the rest of her life, at all times when he had a house' (Boswell, 1751). Johnson admired her conversational

powers, and bore patiently with her ill humours.   Other inmates were Mrs. Desmoulins, the penniless daughter of an old Stafford-shire friend ; Robert Levett, a medical practitioner in a very small way among the London poor; the negro servant Frank ; and Hodge the cat, for whom Johnson used to buy oysters.

89. Johnson's views are no doubt extreme; but they may warn us against supposing the verdicts of Macaulay and other Whig historians to be above criticism.   Elsewhere Johnson concedes to William III 'the resplendent qualities of steady resolution and personal courage.'

It was George II who was accused of suppressing his father's will.

90. Books were sold unbound or in a temporary casing. The buyer usually employed his own binder, who cut, and often gilded, the leaves.   On examination of a sheet of an uncut octavo it will be seen that of the sixteen pages four can be read without hindrance, eight with difficulty and only in part four are wholly inaccessible.

92. Johnson's notorious prejudice against Scotchmen was partly caused by his dislike of those Scotchmen who, after the union of the parliaments, came to London to seek their fortune (often under the protection of a great Scottish noble such as Lord Bute).   They offended Johnson by their ' extreme nation-ality ' and clannish spirit.   Reasonable Scots will agree that this charge is still not without foundation.   His famous and bitterly resented ' remark upon the nakedness of the country, from its being denuded of trees, was made after having travelled two hundred miles along the eastern coast, where certainly trees are not to be found near the road ; and he said it was " a map of the road " which he gave ' (Boswell, 1775).

99. Johnson is contrasting the English Midlands with the Western Islands.

104. The grey, or Norwegian, rat is said to have almost exterminated the black, or English, rat ; which, however, is still to be seen on the West coast and in the islands.

110. *Cowley* : Abraham Cowley (1618-67).   Old editions are still common.   Johnson considered his *Life of Cowley* ' as the

best of the whole, on account of the dissertation which it contains on the *Metaphysical Poets'* (Boswell).

Hurd: Richard Hurd (1720-1808), Bishop of Worcester. His *Letters on Chivalry and Romance* (1762) are reprinted in the *Oxford Library of Prose and Poetry*.

Flatman: Thomas Flatman (1637-88), a minor poet.

112. *A journey to Italy* with the Thrales had been arranged, but was postponed in consequence of their son's death; it never took place.

117. The *Poems, supposed to have been written at Bristol, by Thomas Rowley, and others, in the fifteenth century*, should be read in Tyrwhitt's edition, or in the Oxford reprint of his (third, 1778) edition; which has an introduction on the *Rowley* controversy and some additions to Tyrwhitt's glossary. Tyrwhitt proved the poems spurious by his discovery that all Chatterton's archaisms were taken straight out of Speght's *Chaucer*, Kersey's *Dictionarium Anglo-Britannicum*, and Bailey's *Universal Etymological Dictionary*. But people who have been imposed upon are always unwilling to allow that they have been fooled; and many persisted in 'the resolution to say again what has once been said' (184).

Thomas Tyrwhitt (1730-86), was a notable Greek scholar, and produced an edition of Aristotle's *Poetics* which is still valuable. He was one of the first to apply (in his editions of Chaucer and Chatterton) to the editing of English texts the principles of criticism which had been long familiar to classical scholars.

120. *John Wilkes* (1727-97), demagogue and profligate, editor of the periodical political pamphlet *The North Briton*, in which ministers were lampooned, and hero of the famous Middlesex election. He was always popular, and became at last prosperous. Johnson in *The False Alarm* and Wilkes in *The North Briton* had attacked each other with savage invective.

121. *Old Cibber:* Colley Cibber (1671-1757), poet laureate, and hero of Pope's *Dunciad*. His plays and birthday odes are now seldom disinterred, but his *Apology for his Life* is still good reading.

122. The following version of the Epitaph is taken from Forster's *Life of Goldsmith*:

OF OLIVER GOLDSMITH—
Poet, Naturalist, Historian,
who left scarcely any kind of writing
untouched,
and touched nothing that he did not adorn :
Whether smiles were to be stirred
or tears,
commanding our emotions, yet a gentle master :
In genius lofty, lively, versatile,
in style weighty, clear, engaging—
The memory in this monument is cherished
by the love of Companions,
the faithfulness of Friends
the reverence of Readers.
He was born in Ireland,
at a place called Pallas,
(in the parish) of Forney, (and county) of Longford,
on the 29th Nov. 1731.
Trained in letters at Dublin.
Died in London,
4th April, 1774.

if he can distinguish. Goldsmith, however, did his best. He not only studied Buffon's Natural History, he also visited the Zoo, where he took the measurements of the tiger 'as well as I could, through the bars'.

123. *mutual friend*: a very old mistake.

Journey to Corsica should be *Account of Corsica.*

As there are many things to admire in both performances. In the early editions, and probably in all reprints, these words are printed as belonging to the next sentence. Sir Alexander doubtless meant to give a reason for putting the two books together on his shelves.

papadendrion : ' He means to imply, I suppose, that Johnson was the father of plantations• (Birkbeck Hill). *papadendrion* is very barbarous Greek.

124. Learned books were very often published by subscription. The author issued *Proposals,* and gave *receipts* to his subscribers, who were entitled to a copy of the book on publication. Sometimes

part of the price was paid in advance, the rest on delivery. If the plan fell through the money was presumably returned ; but Johnson told a pleasant story of one Cooke, who 'lived twenty years on a translation of Plautus, for which he was always taking subscriptions.' (Boswell, *Tour to the Hebrides.*)

125. *Literary Property.* See note on 75.

126. See 21. The tide of barbarism in the Dark Ages stopped short of the coast of Ireland, which became one of the last refuges of the old civilization. Irish scribes have preserved for us many of the writings of antiquity.

127. This gorgeous piece owes part of its matchless harmony to the alternation of slow monosyllabic rhythms with smooth and rapid endings : of *to be at once amiable and great, to make haste, how Kings should live* ; with *favour of your Majesty* (–◡◡◡ –◡◡), *national interest* (–◡◡ –◡◡), *tribute of reverence* (–◡◡ –◡◡), *how they should be honoured* (–◡◡◡ –◡), *Subject and Servant* (–◡◡ –◡). . See note on 144. The voice rises and pauses on *how Kings should live* ; falls away in rapid cadence on *how they should be honoured.*

Dedication †. Boswell indicated by an *asterisk** writings which Johnson acknowledged to his friends ; and by a *dagger* † those which were ascertained to be his by internal evidence.

131. *Miss Aikin* (Mrs. Barbauld) wrote, in imitation of the *Rambler*, an essay *On Romances, an Imitation.*

133. *idea.* Johnson used *idea* as Locke did ; but both were historically wrong. The Platonic idea was an abstract notion, not an image.

134. Johnson's passionate hatred of the slave-trade was the cause of his animosity against the Americans.

135. See 110.

138. *Martin.* See 37.

141. *Dr. Young:* Edward Young (1683-1765) author of *Night Thoughts*, a didactic and philosophic poem in blank verse, at one time much admired.

142. *The Traveller.* Johnson told Boswell that he wrote only some ten lines of *The Traveller* and four of *The Deserted Village*, including the last lines of both. (Boswell, 1766).

143 γηράσκειν : ' to grow old, still learning.'

144. *Potter's Aeschylus* is a forgotten work.   Few translators
have had any success in their attempts to render Aeschylus into
English verse.   Browning's *Agamemnon* is often unintelligible
without reference to the Greek, and is seldom poetry.

Pope's *Homer* was extravagantly lauded in its time, and
has since been extravagantly abused.   Charles Lamb preferred
the Elizabethan Chapman. ˙ Both are very unlike Homer.
The Greekless reader may best get an idea of the *Iliad* and
Odyssey from the prose translation by the late Andrew Lang
and his collaborators (published by Macmillan).   They lack
the thunder of the verse, and are perhaps over-Biblical in
phrase ; but they are accurate, and free from the false flourishes
of metrical translations.

heroick is the same as *epic*.   Originally it was so called
because it celebrated the deeds of the *Heroes*—a hero or demigod
was the son of a god and a mortal mother (Hercules) or of a
goddess and a mortal father (Achilles).   The dactylic hexameter of
the Homeric poems was called by the Greeks the *heroic rhythm.*

Numerous prose.   Pope ' lisp'd in *numbers* ' ; similarly
numerous means what we now commonly call metrical or
rhythmical.

The laws of classical numerous prose, which had been long
forgotten, have been recovered in recent years, and have been
traced down to the Middle Ages, when Papal Bulls were written
according to fixed metrical rules.   English literature inherited
the tradition, and these rules were often unconsciously observed.
The regular form of a sentence ending of this kind is *an accented
syllable* followed by *two unaccented syllables* (–◡◡, a dactyl) or
by *three unaccented syllables* (–◡◡◡), which are themselves
followed by a *trochaic cadence*, –◡ or –◡◡ or –◡ –◡.

The *Iona* passage (131) is an admirable example of classical
rhythm in English prose ; e. g. il*lustrious island* (–◡◡ –◡),
Cale*donian region* (–◡◡ –◡), *roving barbarians* (–◡◡ –◡◡),
benefits of knowledge (–◡◡◡ –◡), *blessings of religion* (–◡◡◡–◡),
dignity of thinking beings (–◡◡◡ –◡ –◡), *ruins of Iona*
(–◡◡◡ –◡).

Johnson was wrong if he said that Sir William Temple first 'gave cadence to English Prose.' The *Book of Common Prayer* contains on every page examples of the classical rhythm (The Scripture *moveth us in sundry places* —ᴗᴗ —ᴗ —ᴗ to acknowledge and confess our *manifold sins and wickedness* —ᴗᴗ —ᴗ —ᴗᴗ and that we should not dis*semble nor cloke them* —ᴗᴗ —ᴗ before the face of Almighty God our *Heavenly Father* —ᴗᴗ —ᴗ). The best English prose of the seventeenth century is full of these cadences.

An account of the mediaeval *cursus*, as these rules are called, may be read in Prof. A. C. Clark's *Cursus in Mediaeval and Vulgar Latin*; and discussions of the same cadences, and of different, non-classical rhythms, as used in English, in the same writer's *Prose Rhythm in English* and in articles by Prof. Elton and Mr. D. S. MacColl in *Essays and Studies by Members of the English Association*, 1913 and 1914 (all Clarendon Press).

or an insignificant word. 'A tedious person', says Ben Jonson, 'is one a man would leap a steeple from, gallop down any steep hill to avoid him.' This may be rendered into the correct English of the eighteenth century somewhat as follows : ' To avoid an encounter with a tedious person, a man would leap from the tallest steeple, or gallop down the most perilous declivity' (the jingle of *steep* and *steeple* would be avoided). But when Ben Jonson goes on : 'He opened an entry into a fair room, but shut it again presently. I spake to him of garlick he answered asparagus'—translation becomes impossible.

The neglect by the eighteenth century of Elizabethan and early seventeenth-century literature is often exaggerated. The dramatists indeed, except Shakespeare and Jonson, whose collected plays had been printed in folio, were little read; and the minor poets and pamphleteers, whose names at least are now familiar from the light which they throw on Shakespeare, were hardly known. On the other hand such books as Sidney's *Arcadia*, Raleigh's *History of the World*, and the English works of Bacon, were more read then than now. It is however true that the earlier writers suffered comparative neglect at a time when the literature of the Restoration and of the age of Queen Anne was far better known than it is to-day ; and this neglect is reflected in such a book as Boswell's *Life*. Sir Thomas -Browne, whose life Johnson wrote, is mentioned occasionally ; and there are references to Massinger, Overbury, Coriat, and a few more ; but by most men of letters these writers were either forgotten or recalled as curiosities. To this general neglect Dodsley's collecttion of old plays was a notable exception. Johnson himself 'loved the old black-letter books'. On the island of Col he sat on a hill-side reading *Gataker on Lots*.

The collection of poetry to which Johnson's *Lives* were prefaces is instructive in this connexion. It was originally intended to begin with Chaucer, and we do not know why the design was altered ; Johnson had no responsibility for it. But it is significant that a collection of the writings 'of the most eminent English poets', which makes it appear that English poetry begins with Cowley, should have been published by the associated booksellers of London and, as appears, received without protest.

150. This Edwards, 'a decent-looking elderly man in grey clothes, and a wig of many curls', had been at Pembroke with Johnson ; but they had lived in London for forty years without seeing each other, till one day they met on their way from church.

156. *Mr. Allan Ramsay*. This was Ramsay the younger, a painter of portraits. His father, Allan Ramsay the elder, wrote *The Gentle Shepherd*, a Scottish pastoral.

he will believe anything. It was a common notion—which Boswell earnestly refutes—that Johnson was foolishly credulous where his prejudices were engaged ; that, for instance, he was ready to credit any story of ghosts.

158. Johnson did not talk of *runts* from choice ; for he complained to Boswell of his old friend Dr. Taylor : 'Sir, I love him ; but I do not love him more ; my regard for him does not increase. As it is said in the Apocrypha, "his talk is of bullocks"' (Boswell, 1777).

163. *eclipsed, not extinguished* : Shelley, *Adonais* :
>   The splendours of the firmament of time
>   May be eclipsed, but are extinguished not.

166. See 75.

167. *Dr. Lawrence* : Thomas Lawrence, Johnson's physician and friend.

168. *nec, ut soles:* 'we shall hear you jest no more'; from the famous poem by the Emperor Hadrian, *Dying, to his Soul*, which begins

Animula, vagula, blandula.

173. ' Here lies Nolly Goldsmith, for shortness called Noll,
      Who wrote like an angel, but talk'd like poor Poll.'
(Garrick.)

175. *brutality of insolence.* The reference is to Milton's controversial pamphlets.

fallen on evil days : Paradise Lost, vii. 25 :
          though fall'n on evil dayes,
   On evil dayes though fall'n, and evil tongues :
   In darkness, and with dangers compast round.

176. *a friend of his son :* Herbert Croft, whose *Life of Young* Johnson abridged and included in his *Lives*.

180. *Bluestocking* is thus defined by the *Oxford Dictionary* ; 'originally one who frequented Mrs. Montague's assemblies; thence transferred sneeringly to any woman showing a taste for learning. Much used by reviewers of the first quarter of the nineteenth century ; but now, from the general change of opinion on the education of women, nearly abandoned'. Johnson was fond of the society of learned ladies, and thought well of their literature. Several of the *Ramblers* were written for him by women.

181. *making provision :* Preface to the *Dictionary* : ' Much of my life has been lost under the pressures of disease ; much has been trifled away ; and much has always been spent in provision for the day that was passing over me '.

183. See 17.

184. *Edmond Malone* (1741-1812), a great scholar and anti-quary. For his share in revising and editing the *Life of Johnson* see note on p. xii. His Variorum edition of Shakespeare, first published in 1790, was the culmination of the long series of editions which began with Rowe's and Pope's. The standard edition of Malone's *Shakespeare* is that edited by James Boswell the younger and published in 1821. ' This is generally

reckoned to be the best edition of our great Dramatist '(Watt, *Bibliotheca Britannica*, 1824). Another of Malone's great services to literature was his superb collection of early editions, particularly of the dramatists, part of which now forms the Malone Collection in the Bodleian Library.

Chatterton. See 117.

185. Exhortations to thrift, when as commonly happens they are admonitions addressed to poor men by rich men, are seldom impressive. Johnson's solemn warnings, coming from a generous man who had been miserably poor, and never became rich, have a very different stamp.

189. *Ingenium ingens :* ' a mighty mind hidden in an uncouth body' (Horace, *Satires* i. 3. 33).

190. *George Buchanan* (1506–82) of the University of St. Andrews, a poet and politician of Queen Mary's time. He was tutor to James the Sixth and First. In Scotland his best-known work was, and is, the *History of Scotland*; but his Latin poetry had European fame. *Baptistes, seu Tragedia de Calumnia* was printed at Frankfort ; *Tragediae Sacrae Jephthes et Baptistes*, at Paris and Geneva; and of the *Paraphrasis Psalmorum Davidis Poetica* editions appeared in the sixteenth and seventeenth centuries at London, Edinburgh, Antwerp, Amsterdam, and many other places.

191. *Maurice Morgann. The Essay on the Dramatic Character of Sir John Falstaff* (1777 ; reprinted in *Oxford Library of Prose and Poetry*) was undertaken for a wager, and in a spirit of deliberate paradox ; but it contains, in digression, admirable serious criticism.

Derrick's poetry, such as it was, made him *King of Bath*, as the Master of the Ceremonies there was called. See Goldsmith's *Life of Richard Nash.*

For *Smart* see 26.

198. That Milton wrote poor sonnets is a view that may surprise ; but, as it is stated by Miss Hannah More and accepted by Johnson, we must suppose it to have been the common opinion.

205. *Te teneam*: ' When I am dying, may my failing hand hold yours ' (Tibullus, i. 1. 60).

INDEX

Printed in England at the Oxford University Press

CPSIA information can be obtained
at www.ICGtesting.com
Printed in the USA
LVOW07s0702270917
550236LV00018B/430/P